Together and Different

Malcolm Torry is Team Rector in the East Greenwich Team Ministry and co-ordinator of a multi faith chaplaincy at The O2 on the Greenwich Peninsula, London.

Sarah Thorley is an experienced specialist in religious education in schools. She is the author of the Words and Pictures series of books on world religions that are widely used in schools, and is a member of the Standing Advisory Council for Religious Education in Lambeth.

Also published by Canterbury Press

The Parish: People, Place and Ministry – A Theological and Practical Exploration
Editor: Malcolm Torry

'a timely, stimulating and, above all, encouraging account of parish ministry by practitioners who clearly believe in it, enjoy it and are good at it . . . warmly recommended'. *Church Times*

Diverse Gifts: Varieties of Lay and Ordained Ministry in the Church and Community
Editor: Malcolm Torry

'a treasure trove of pastoral insights . . . those involved in, or training for, any kind of ministry should find it useful'. *CR Quarterly*

Ordained Local Ministry: A New Shape for Ministry in the Church of England
Editors: Malcolm Torry and Jeffrey Heskins

A landmark volume and the first in-depth study of this contemporary model of priesthood.

Regeneration and Renewal: The Church in New and Changing Communities
Editor: Malcolm Torry

'The contributors to this volume identify a host of issues, tensions, and contradictions within the processes of renewal and regeneration . . . the energy, vision, resourcefulness, and faithfulness that characterise many churches working in this area.' *Church Times*

Together and Different

*Christians engaging with people
of other faiths*

Edited by
Malcolm Torry
and
Sarah Thorley

CANTERBURY
PRESS
Norwich

First published in 2008 by the Canterbury Press Norwich
(a publishing imprint of Hymns Ancient & Modern Limited,
a registered charity)
13–17 Long Lane, London EC1A 9PN

www.scm-canterburypress.co.uk

British Library Cataloguing in Publication data

A catalogue record for this book is available
from the British Library

ISBN 978-1-85311-881-4

Typeset by Regent Typesetting, London
Printed and bound by
CPI William Clowes Beccles NR34 7TL

Contents

Foreword

This important book brings together stories of the practical, creative and open-hearted engagement of Christians with people of other faiths, in our contemporary society, together with invaluable reflections and comments from the colleagues of different faiths with whom they have shared these experiences. These accounts of what has been achieved in practical terms are accompanied by thoughtful reflections on what has been learned as a result and by a set of helpful guidelines for inter faith engagement of this kind.

The accounts come from many different settings, including schools, hospitals, a church in a multi faith area and regeneration initiatives. But the common theme is one of encounter and engagement as Christians work through the steps that need to be taken in order to do justice to the greater religious diversity across this country, and to respond to this, not only in different institutional settings, but also in the face of external events like the London bombings of July 2007. It is particularly valuable to have detailed accounts of what this involves in practical terms: it is this kind of sensitive and careful engagement with one another that is required if we are to develop a truly cohesive, while plural, society.

The greater religious diversity which we encounter does not just result from the arrival over the last few decades of substantial numbers of migrants linked to a variety of the world's major religious traditions – and coming from different strands within these – but also from more varied patterns of belief among both those who understand themselves to be religious and those who do not.

The hallmarks of the stories that the authors tell are a deep integrity, rooted in commitment to their own Christian faith, yet open to the demands and insights to be found now at every turn in our society. There is, throughout, a clear-eyed recognition that we must acknowledge with integrity the genuine differences that exist between different faiths and beliefs, but at the same time seek the common ground wherever and whenever we can find this. This is not easy work; it is hard and challenging. But there is a clear sense too of the enrichment and fulfilment which it has brought to those engaged in it.

As the editors of this volume say on behalf its authors: 'We have written these stories because we have all been changed by the events which we record.' The horizons of the writers have been expanded and the understanding of their own faith, as well as that of others, has been deepened. The reflections from those of other faiths underline that for them, too, the same challenges and potential for enrichment are present. Lasting friendships have been made.

The theme of mutuality – mutual engagement, mutual help and mutual enrichment – runs throughout the book. It is one that will be of great value to those who are finding themselves drawn into similar situations. But it is full of insights for us all as we reflect on the implications for public policy and practice and the living of our personal lives.

There is great treasure to be found within these pages. It is a thought-provoking book but one which I hope will also prompt *action*: action inspired by faith and by commitment to the common good.

Brian Pearce OBE
Director of the Inter Faith Network for the United Kingdom,
1987–2007

Acknowledgements

We are grateful to all those people who have contributed to this book, and particularly to the authors, to all those who have written responses to the chapters, and to all those who have been willing to talk to us or correspond with us as we have prepared our chapters. We are grateful to those who have commented on our drafts; to the Ven. Michael Ipgrave for information for Chapter 1; to Brian Pearce for his Foreword; and particularly to Christine Smith of Canterbury Press for her enthusiasm for this project.

There are often a number of possible spellings for transliterations from Arabic and from languages of the Indian subcontinent. We have generally relied on the spellings given in John Bowker, 1999, *The Oxford Dictionary of World Religions*, Oxford: Oxford University Press; and we have also relied on this reference work for some of the meanings listed in the Glossary at Appendix 3.

The Contributors

Helen Bailey originally trained as a journalist and now teaches English to speakers of other languages. Her particular concern is for intercultural understanding and global justice, with a focus on the Middle East. She has travelled widely and lived, worked and studied in three continents, teaching Palestinian refugees in Beirut and running international youth projects in Brussels. Prior to teaching she spent some years in the major development agencies of Oxfam, Christian Aid and Cafod. She has a 'home' in an ethnically diverse Anglican church in Tulse Hill, South London, where she strives to live a simple life.

Alan Gadd was ordained an Anglican priest in 1972 and was a Minister in Secular Employment, working in the Meteorological Office on Numerical Weather Prediction, until 1995. There followed ten years as a parish priest at All Saints' Church, Battersea Park, during which time he had a prominent role in the inter faith activities of the Diocese of Southwark. In 2004 Alan joined the Committee of the South London Inter Faith Group, and he has served as the organisation's Secretary since 2006.

Georgiana Heskins is an Anglican priest and is a hospital chaplain and an honorary theatre and cathedral chaplain. She has taught biblical studies and theology in various contexts, including ordination and reader training and in two secondary schools. She is an Examining Chaplain to the Bishop of Southwark and is secretary of the Greenwich Multi Faith Forum.

Maureen Mullally practised as a barrister specialising in family law for 27 years, after bringing up her family of seven children. She now works as a member of the UK College of Family Mediators, helping divorcing and separating couples to negotiate their own solutions to problems relating to their children, their finances and their property. Maureen has written several books for non-lawyers explaining family law in understandable terms. She writes a weekly column on family matters in the Roman Catholic newspaper *The Universe*. She is a member of the Child Protection Commissions for the Roman Catholic Archdiocese of Southwark and for the Jesuit Order.

Alison Price trained for ordination at Westcott House, Cambridge, and served as a curate from 1995 at All Saints' with St Margaret's, Upper Norwood, in the diocese of Southwark. She remained in the diocese and became the incumbent of St Barnabas', Mitcham, in a culturally and religiously diverse community. In September 2007 Alison resigned her living as vicar following the birth of her son. She has moved to Southampton, also a lively and culturally and religiously diverse place. She now describes herself as a mother in Holy Orders.

Catriona Robertson is a fan of the theologian Howard Thurman who wrote, 'Do not ask what the world needs: ask what brings you alive, because what the world needs is people who are alive.' Catriona is co-founder of Clapham and Stockwell Faith Forum, enjoys travelling, and lives in South London with her husband and two teenage children.

Sarah Thorley has lived for 23 years in Brixton, and is a member of her local Anglican church. She has been involved with the South London Inter Faith Group (SLIFG) for twenty-one years and has personal contacts with many of the faith communities in South London. She has recently produced a report for the SLIFG about multi faith South London. Sarah is a part-time teacher of religious education and of children with special educational needs, and a member of Lambeth SACRE (Standing Advisory Council for Religious Education). She has written a series of books on world religions which are widely used in schools.

Malcolm Torry is Team Rector in the East Greenwich Team Ministry, Vicar of St George's, Westcombe Park, and co-ordinator of a multi faith chaplaincy at The O2 on the Greenwich Peninsula. Before ordination he worked for the Department of Health and Social Security. Following ordination he was curate at St Matthew's, Southwark, at the Elephant and Castle; then curate at Christ Church, Southwark, and industrial chaplain with the South London Industrial Mission; and then Vicar of St Catherine's, Hatcham, at New Cross. He is married and has three children.

Alison Tyler is an Anglican priest who lives in South London and is an Honorary Chaplain at Southwark Cathedral. She is the Learning and Development Officer for Prison Service Chaplaincy. She worked for over twenty years as a Probation Officer involved in running alcohol education and sex offender treatment programmes, both in and out of prison. She was ordained in 1995 and since 1999 has been a Prison Chaplain in Brixton, Wandsworth and Wormwood Scrubs prisons and in Feltham Young Offenders Institution. Alison is the Spiritual Director of Cursillo in the Diocese of London, a member of the Court of Sion College, and a member of the Society of Catholic Priests. She is married to Paddy Costigan and they have two adult daughters.

1 Together and Different

Christians engaging with people of other faiths

MALCOLM TORRY AND SARAH THORLEY

Jesus said, 'With what can we compare the kingdom of God, or what parable will we use for it? It is like a mustard seed, which, when sown upon the ground, is the smallest of all the seeds on earth; yet when it is sown it grows up and becomes the largest of all shrubs, and puts forth large branches, so that the birds of the air can make nests in its shade.'

Mark 4.30–32

If the People of the Book accept the true faith and keep from evil, We will pardon them their sins and admit them to the gardens of delight. If they observe the Torah and the Gospel and what is revealed to them from Allah, they shall be given abundance from above and from beneath.

The Holy Qur'an, Sura 5.66[1]

About this book

The purpose of this book is to share the experiences of Christians engaging with people of other faiths at grassroots level and to bring to light some 'good news' stories of religion.

Here you will find a Christian and a Muslim school linking up; you will meet multi faith chaplaincy teams on a construction site, in a hospital, and in a prison; you will experience a multi faith funeral and a multi faith women's group; you will witness a Faith Forum responding to a crisis in a synagogue, Christians learning from a Hindu teacher, and Muslims learning from a Christian teacher; you will encounter Christians and Buddhists sharing sacred space together; and you will journey with a group of Christians to stay with Sikh families in India.

We believe that these stories will be relevant not just to Christians but to people of all faiths. We also hope the book will be of interest to people who have no particular faith allegiance, whatever their attitude is to religion. Increasingly, we all live and work alongside people with a whole spectrum of belief, and often of no belief, and the need for extended friendship and understanding has never been more important.

So often the reporting of relationships between people of different faiths is negative, and sometimes it is distorted and inaccurate. The media don't usually regard good things happening as newsworthy. That's one of the reasons for this book. Each of our stories tells of a positive and creative engagement with people from one or more other faiths, which sometimes arises out of a common need, sometimes from a perceived opportunity, sometimes as part of the challenge of a work situation, and sometimes from a sense of vocation. It's not all easy and things don't always run smoothly, so these aren't simply 'feel-good' stories – they also relate the difficult aspects of forming relationships. We have all been changed by the events that we record.

All our stories are from South London, within about sixteen miles of the River Thames. In the twelve boroughs of South London, where we all live, there are at least seven Sikh gurdwaras, thirteen Hindu temples, a Jain temple, twenty-six mosques, nine Buddhist temples, eleven synagogues, several Baha'i groups, and innumerable churches of various denominations. We know of twenty-two inter faith or multi faith groups or forums with varying constitutions and objectives, some of which are independent and some local council initiatives. Our stories are but glimpses of what is going on in this area.[2] There are excellent inter faith initiatives happening in other parts of the country and, indeed, all over the world,[3] but we have written about what we know. We hope that our stories will say something to you in your particular situation, whether you are Christian, or of another religion, or of no religious allegiance. We hope that you will be encouraged to tell your own stories, and, if nothing much is happening in your area, we hope that this book will energise you to act where you are.

To create this book, each contributor was approached by the editors and asked to prepare a brief summary of a chapter. Once that was agreed, each author wrote a complete draft of his or her own chapter, and these were circulated to all the authors. This was quite a step of trust as most of us didn't know each other. We all met together for a day to comment constructively on one another's work and consider the content for the concluding chapter. An extra valuable dimension of this book is the responses and reflections following each chapter, written by one or more of the people of other faiths who were significantly involved in the story. It has been a privilege to work with these people and to have their wisdom and input, and it was a pleasure to meet together for a meal and discussion before the content of the book was finalised.

This book is not an objective survey or analysis. It is written on the basis of the authors' own experiences and their consultations with others in the places they are writing about and elsewhere. Neither does it claim to be a theological exploration, although sometimes events and situations do give rise to theological reflection within a chapter. Our task has been to provide some raw material on which others will be able to base their own reflections, both theological and practical. There are other books that provide surveys, analysis and theology, but, as far as we know, there is no other book of people's first-hand experiences quite like those recorded in this book. We hope that it will be a useful resource.

Motivation

Why do Christians engage with people of other faiths? The stories recounted here suggest that a wide variety of motives are at work.

First and foremost, Christians have the example of Jesus to follow. Jesus related across religious boundaries to Samaritans and Gentiles. We too are bidden to relate across the religious boundaries of our own time.

Jesus commanded us to 'love our neighbours'[4] and the Scriptures which he read bid us to 'love the stranger'.[5] Here is an imperative to reach out and get to know our neighbours, to learn about and understand one another's religions, and in the process to deepen our understanding of our own beliefs and practices.

Another motivation is to make a contribution to more peaceful and coherent communities. Working together, across faith divisions, we can better serve multi faith communities, better serve people in need, and create hope for a society in which integration and difference are both valued and sought. People of faith need to work together for mutual support in a secular, materialist and sometimes anti-religious world. People of faith need to work together locally so that they may be able to withstand the impact of national and international crises that have a religious dimension. It's in a crisis that relationships of trust between people are so essential – so it's before the crisis arises that they need to be built.

Often, in our now global world, there is a personal or family motivation for getting involved. It may be that our job or our holiday takes us to an Islamic country, our colleagues at work are of other faiths, or as parents we are meeting parents of other faiths at the school gate. The corner shop proprietors or the local solicitor may be Hindu. Our hospital surgeon or garage mechanic may be Sikh. We don't even have to live in a religiously diverse area. There is nowhere we can be isolated and nowhere that inter faith learning is not needed. Television and the internet both bring other religions into our homes and make the necessary learning more possible. It may be that our daughter is at university and wants to marry a Hindu or our brother-in-law is Jewish. Our son might go off with an unusual sect. There's a conversation over a meal or in the pub about terrorism . . . We shall always wish we were more prepared, more knowledgeable, and more at ease with our fellow human beings of other faiths.

You will no doubt discover other motivations for inter faith engagement, both in our stories and from your own experience. Above all, we have found that engagement interesting, challenging, enriching, enjoyable and fun.

Attitude

True dialogue must mean meeting on equal terms, with an open mind and mutual respect. Talking and working together reveals practices and values which we have in common and also practices and values which we don't, and we relate to each other corporately and individually through our differences just as much as through our similarities. Although we share a common humanity, our religions are not 'all the same really': they each contain their own distinctiveness and wisdom.

There is a proper Christian desire to share and to recommend the Christian faith, just as other faith communities will share and recommend their own faiths, but a dead end is reached very quickly if either side detects any kind of coercion or ulterior motive. Honesty and clarity really matter here.

Terminology

For the purposes of this book, we take 'inter faith' to mean relationship building between the faiths (for instance, through dialogue) and we take 'multi faith' to mean working together on joint projects (such as chaplaincy). It's not clear cut, however, as 'multi faith' can also refer to an area or a presence, inter faith activity will often lead to multi faith activity, and multi faith activity will often have inter faith consequences. After some discussion, the authors of this book agreed to use the forms 'inter faith' and 'multi faith' rather than 'interfaith', 'multifaith', 'interfaith' or 'multi-faith', in order to avoid any idea that a new interfaith or multifaith movement, being an amalgam of religions, was being implied or intended.

Don't look away

The message of this book is that there is an urgency to engage with people of other faith communities. We never know what crisis lies around the corner, and when crises arise it would be so much better if we had already made the connections. Wherever we are, unexpected opportunities for creative inter faith and multi faith engagement are there if we can but see them: if we can seize the moment, take the risk, tread new ground, push our boundaries, and be surprised – instead of looking the other way. So much can open up in terms of new friendships, greater understanding of the world, peace in our communities, a deepening of our own spiritual journeys, and generally a deeper enjoyment of the rich diversity of humanity.

Further reading

Barbara Butler, 2006, *Living with Faith: Journeys towards trust, friendship and justice*, Peterborough: Inspire.
Siriol Davies, 2007, *An Evaluation of Different Models of Inter Faith Activity*, London: South London Inter Faith Group.

Sarah Thorley, 2007, *Improved Understanding of South London's Multi Faith Situation*, London: South London Inter Faith Group.

Andrew Wingate, 2005, *Celebrating Difference, Staying Faithful*, London: Darton Longman & Todd.

Notes

1 *The Koran*, 1974, translated by N. J. Dawood, fourth revised edition, Harmondsworth: Penguin, p. 393.

2 Sarah Thorley, 2007, *Improved Understanding of South London's Multi Faith Situation*, London: South London Inter Faith Group: available from South London Inter Faith Group, 24 Holmewood Gardens, London SW2 3RS.

3 In Leicester ministers of different faiths have trained together; the St Ethelburga's Centre for Reconciliation in the City of London has an exciting and ground-breaking multi faith programme; and there are projects to encourage young people of different faiths to relate to each other, for instance, Scripture Union's media project to enable Christian and Muslim young people to explore perceptions of themselves and of each other through making video presentations. There are many bridge-building projects throughout the country (and projects called 'Building Bridges' in Pendle and Burnley); and there is an increasing number of exchange or linking projects to enable children in single faith schools to get to know each other. Both in this country and in other countries the organisation Christians Aware facilitates encounters between Christians and people of other faiths; and on a broader scale Churches and communions have created guidelines – based on experience – to help Christians to relate to people of other faiths (see the further reading list for references). For an example of guidelines on inter faith work, see the Anglican Communion's Network for Inter Faith Concerns, http://nifcon.anglicancommunion.org/index.cfm, and particularly the 'Guidelines for Inter Faith Encounter in the Churches of the Porvoo Communion': http://nifcon.anglicancommunion.org/work/guidelines/docs/porvoo.cfm. For an example of faiths working together to create guidelines for inter faith activity, see the guidelines created by the Interfaith Network UK: www.interfaith.org.uk/pcode.htm.

4 Matthew 22.39.

5 Leviticus 19.34.

2 Learning Together

Christian and Muslim school exchanges

SARAH THORLEY

with a response by Firdos Qazi

Jesus said: 'Blessed are the peacemakers . . .'

Matthew 5.9

You shall surely guide them to the right path: the path of Allah, to whom belongs all that the heavens and the earth contain. All things shall in the end return to Him.

The Holy Qur'an, from Sura 42[1]

'Miss, they wear jeans under those long robes!' This was one of many discoveries made between pupils at a Church of England and a Muslim primary school in South London, where regular exchanges have been taking place in recent years.

It all started when I struck up a friendship with the head teacher of the Muslim school, Firdos Qazi. I needed a Muslim teacher to scrutinise a book for Religious Education I was writing and she was valiantly managing 400 children and staff in a partially converted old cinema building. We met several times and were soon into deep discussions about all the topical religious issues of the day. We've been to each other's homes at weekends and it has been wonderful to find someone with whom I could raise questions about the most difficult and sensitive subjects. I have learned a great deal from her and clarified many of my own ideas.

I teach at Holy Trinity, a school in Brixton with 400 mostly Christian pupils from a variety of cultural backgrounds, including many of African-Caribbean heritage and many whose families are from Africa: Nigeria and Ghana in particular. Usually there are three or four Muslim families in the school and a handful of Hindu children.

The neighbourhood is very cosmopolitan with a cross section of social backgrounds. Large council estates stand back to back with big Victorian terraced family homes, many of which are owned by families who came from the Caribbean and have lived here for more than 50 years. There are children in the school with professional parents and some with relatives in Brixton Prison. I live near the school and I'm friendly with a Muslim family whose father is a psychiatrist and with a Muslim single mother who struggles to pay for her children's school outings.

In the adjacent street is a Caribbean Hindu temple which was established in 1972 and welcomes visits from Holy Trinity School when the children are studying Hinduism. There are Orthodox and Liberal Jewish synagogues within easy reach of the school, both of which are very friendly and are regularly visited by Holy Trinity pupils and other local schools.

The church to which the school is attached is of an evangelical tradition. The present vicar, who lived for eight years in Egypt, is very knowledgeable about Islam and has encouraged and taken part in our exchange visits. The school staff range from committed Christians of various traditions to those with very little church affiliation and some who call themselves atheist. It is, nevertheless, a strong, forward-looking and mutually supportive staff team.

The children are taught about religions other than Christianity. However, there is an ongoing debate about which religions should be taught and at what stage, and about how much time should be given to them. (Similar debates take place in many church and other single faith schools.)[2]

Gatton School, of which Firdos Qazi is the head teacher, is the fourth Muslim school in the country to have become state funded. It is no longer housed in the old Odeon Cinema but in the first purpose-built, state-of-the-art Muslim school building in the UK. It has 400 children and is located within a very ethnically mixed population which includes one of the most vibrant Asian communities in South London, in Tooting. Currently all its pupils are Muslims, from a wide range of countries (Somalia, Middle Eastern Arabic countries, Pakistan and others) with many different first languages. The school governors are committed to an admissions policy of a minimum of 15 per cent of places for local children of other religions (or none), even though a large number of Muslim children are on the waiting list. The staff are not all Muslim and the school takes on a number of trainee teachers, both Muslim and non-Muslim.

'It was a great trip and a real eye-opener. The school staff were very friendly and welcoming. I was surprised to meet a Christian teacher there . . . I hadn't realised this was even a possibility.' (Holy Trinity parent)

Within easy walking distance of Gatton School are churches of all denominations, a Sikh gurdwara, a Hindu temple, the Tooting Islamic Centre where there are secondary schools for boys and girls, a Shi'a Muslim centre – and behind Gatton School is a small, recently built mosque with a golden dome. Religious education taught in the school covers all religions, but there is an extra hour added to the school day which is given to the study of Islam. Apart from that, the curriculum is the same as in any other school – as our children would find out.

Firdos and I don't entirely agree about single faith schools, but when we met in 2002, as we talked and thrashed through all the issues, what we did agree about was that we should work with the reality on the ground, which for us was that we each worked in a single faith school. How could we make the best of this given situation? Indeed, how could we turn this challenge into a positive, creative and enriching experience – for ourselves, for the children, for the staff, and for the parents too?

We decided that year 5 pupils would be a good start: nine- and ten-year-olds who are aware of differences and should already have some knowledge of each other's religions from their religious education learning. Firdos' instinct was that it would be good not to lay on any special programme, nor to spend lots of money, nor even to teach explicitly about religion, but just to let them find out about each other and the other school by joining in with whatever was going on. I agreed.

So the day arrived for our first visit to Gatton. A couple of families had objected, feeling that as a Christian school it wasn't appropriate to be spending time in a Muslim school, so unfortunately we had to leave those children behind. Nothing ever goes completely smoothly – but sometimes setbacks and mistakes can be turned to advantage, as you will see.

The girls and female teachers and accompanying parents brought headscarves and wore trousers or skirts covering their knees. We piled on to the local bus for the 30 minute journey to Tooting. It was immediately quite shocking to see the dark and cramped conditions in which the school operated in the old cinema, but they managed very impressively without complaint and achieved very high academic standards. Within half an hour of arriving, all our children could count to ten in Urdu. That broke the ice and then the Gatton year 5s gave our children a quick quiz on Islam (we had prepared for this). Now it was time to split our children into groups of four and they were whisked off to join classes all around the building; we, the staff and accompanying parents, wouldn't see them again for an hour. Some went to a maths lesson in year 4 (eight- and nine-year-olds), others went to do art with the reception class, others learnt to write Arabic in year 5 (nine- and ten-year-olds), others were doing science with year 6 (ten- and eleven-year-olds), and some played badminton in the hall (the old cinema auditorium).

The visiting adults were taken on a tour of the school. Two or three of their female staff wore the niqab: the face veil which leaves only their eyes showing. They explained to us that when they were in the classroom teaching, they lifted the niqab off their faces, and if male staff wanted to come in they would knock so that the teacher could cover her face first. None of our staff had spoken with a Muslim before, so it was a whole new experience for them.

On the way back on the bus there was a great deal of chatter about how surprisingly like Holy Trinity the teaching was – 'It's just like us, Miss. They were doing graphs too.' 'They speak *English*, Sir.' Some were proudly carrying their name written in Arabic, others had clay pots they had made, and others had Islamic patterns they'd coloured. 'When are they coming back to us?' they wanted to know.

'I had fun skipping and playing badminton and learning how to speak the Arabic way.' (Sherieka, Holy Trinity)

'I liked best when they came to our art sessions because it was really fun and they learned how to write their name in Arabic.' (Al-Haarith, Gatton)

'I liked them coming into our class . . . the purpose is for Muslims and Christians to have a beautiful bond of relation-ships and be friends.' (Zahra, Gatton)

'Two weeks later' was the answer. I spoke to the whole school in Assembly the day before the visit. I knew it would be quite astonishing for our children when thirty Muslim children walked into the school, the girls wearing the long shalwar kameez and their heads covered and many of the boys also wearing 'Islamic' dress, loose trousers and caps or hats; the teachers and accompanying parents also covered from head to foot. It was important to prepare the children and explain how these clothes were worn mainly for reasons of modesty, as the Qur'an decrees, but with variations according to the custom of the country from which each person comes. (Now in their new school building, they have a nicely designed uniform based on the shalwar kameez shape.) I asked the children not to stare rudely, but said it would be fine to ask questions in a friendly way, and no doubt the Muslim children would have plenty of questions too, for instance: 'Why do you wear short skirts?' I reminded them to be friendly and ask our visitors to join in games at playtime. The visit went off very well. They were shy to start with but by the end of break time some of them were swapping mobile phone numbers and email addresses.

So began an exchange each term with the same children meeting up six times in the year.

'I liked playtime best because we could meet up with the children we met last time.' (Aisha, Holy Trinity)

'The benefit is to know a little bit of their religion and to see what it is like in other schools.' (Tasha, Gatton)

The third year I became ambitious. I persuaded Holy Trinity staff to let me set up a 'Learning about Islam Week' in which the whole school would participate. I begged, borrowed and bought posters, books and artefacts from Religious Education Centres and other schools, from libraries and Islamic Centres and from friends, and I assembled an interactive exhibition in the dining hall.

Every afternoon was dedicated to learning about Islam. During the week, staff and pupils from Gatton came in to contribute to assemblies, visited classrooms for discussions and helped our pupils to complete an exhibition trail. The trail included listening to a recording of the call to prayer, working out the times for prayer, learning about the Hajj (pilgrimage), trying on special clothes for the Eid festivals, and the Gatton girls showing our girls how to put on the hijab (head covering) and talking about fasting and charity.

Once again two of our parents refused to allow their children to take part, but to my great delight, half way through the week, one of those parents changed his mind. 'I don't want my daughter growing up with the prejudices that I have,' he said.

A couple of our Muslim parents came and spoke about their faith in the classrooms and I discovered that one of our dinner ladies is Muslim. The year 2 (six- and seven-year-olds) children were amazed when she came to speak to them: 'But she's our dinner lady.' 'Yes, and she's Muslim.' As it happens, she doesn't cover her head (except when praying), so that was another stereotype overturned.

> *Written comments from Holy Trinity year 6 (ten- to eleven-year-olds) at the end of the week:*

> 'Now I value and respect their religion . . . now I think that looking at religions can make you learn something important about yours.' (Remi)

> 'Muslims know the Qur'an by heart. It inspired me to keep the Bible in a safe place and learn at least a verse.' (Darren)

> 'Muslims have taught me about their life and I am willing to tell them mine. I think that Muslims should be treated the way we would like to be treated.' (Sabrina)

> *Feedback questionnaires from Holy Trinity teachers:*

> 'Best aspect was the very open conversation – in year 6 – with the Muslim teacher and children who came into our class.'

> 'Some lovely comments from parents in school reading diaries, about their children's enthusiasm for the week.'

> 'Great that we *celebrated* Islam – not just tolerance or acceptance. Visits by teachers and children from Gatton school was absolutely key.'

The day planned for the schools' joint visit to Southwark Cathedral was 7 July, 2005. That term, Gatton year 5s were learning about

Christianity. Our year 5s were studying Christian symbols and their meanings. We booked in for the Cathedral Education department's 'Signs and Symbols' trail. We would get on our respective buses from Brixton and Tooting and meet at the cathedral at 10 a.m. We arrived but there was no sign of Gatton. We waited and waited. Mobile phone message – their bus couldn't get through and they'd had to turn back. Police car and ambulance sirens. Phone calls revealed that there was some kind of major emergency going on out there. Anxious parents were phoning our school. Of course, we learned later on about the terrible events: the bombs on the bus and underground. We were stranded at the cathedral for three hours until a coach came with a police escort to get us safely back to school. An uncle of one of the Gatton children had been killed by one of the bombs, and our year 5 children signed a card for the family. We said we hoped to have our cathedral trip next term.

Which we certainly did. And we had a great day together. The Cathedral Signs and Symbols trail is excellent and very imaginatively devised, and all the pupils enjoyed it. Our joint picnic didn't work out as we'd originally planned, but became a good learning experience. It was now the month of Ramadan so the Muslim pupils were fasting. They explained to us why they fasted and then went out to watch the boats on the River Thames while we ate our packed lunches. That made quite an impression on our children. Afterwards we all walked along the river bank together with our sketchbooks, stopping at Sir Francis Drake's *Golden Hind* ship and Shakespeare's Globe Theatre and chattering all the way.

We were pleased that the tragic events of two months earlier and the subsequent 'islamophobia' had not prevented us from having our day out together in the end. How important, it seemed, not to allow global and national crises to undermine our local neighbourhood relationships and harmony.

However, one unexpected issue had to be tackled. Half way round the trail the children had been invited to dress up in a range of clerical robes (child sized). Here were Muslim children wearing garments with Christian symbols on them, some of which really did contradict their understanding of 'One God'. Nothing was said at the time, but later that day I thought I should speak to their teacher, Rifat, about it. It was apparent that it had caused considerable debate among the staff and children on the way back to school and heart-searching about whether to say

anything to us about it. Rifat and I talked it through and I said I
would talk to our children and also write to the cathedral saying
'Wonderful day . . .', but mentioning that it's not appropriate for
Muslim children to put on those garments. The following day,
with their class teacher's agreement, I had an in-depth discussion
with our year 5 children. They were really interested and
thoughtful in their responses about which Christian symbols
might be compatible with Islam, and about the oneness of God
and the divinity of Jesus. Was it all right for them to try on the
hijab? Or the white robes for the Hajj? It was a much more meaningful conversation, based on our real experience, than any
book-based discussion would have been.

I've laboured this incident because a further conversation with
Rifat made me feel that we'd sorted it out well and that it really is
important to *talk* about these things. If we hadn't, *they* might
never have gone to the cathedral again or quite trusted our
initiatives, *we* wouldn't have thought about the issues and nor
might the Cathedral Education department, and an otherwise
enriching shared experience might not have been repeated.

Since then the children have visited each other's local mosque
and church – again, not without some controversy. Our children
were learning about Islam so it seemed a good opportunity to
visit Gatton School on a Friday and be able to observe the older
children's fifteen minutes of formal midday prayers in their
prayer hall. Afterwards we would go together to visit the small
adjacent mosque. It was all set up. Letters of consent had come
back from our parents, but at the last minute one of our governors objected very strongly to our children being present at
Muslim prayers. So that part of the visit had to be cancelled.
However, in the event, half a dozen accompanying parents did
attend the prayers, which provided helpful and positive feed-
back. The mosque visit was much enjoyed by pupils, staff and
parents, many of whom hadn't been inside a mosque before.

A few weeks later, we had a constructive meeting at school,
with our vicar and representatives of staff and governors, where
we talked through the distinction between 'being present at and
observing' and 'taking part in [prayers]'. We agreed to write a
clarifying letter to all parents, assuring them that our children
would not be asked to *take part in* any act of prayer or worship
other than Christian. We write up each visit in our weekly
newsletter to parents so that all are aware of the exchanges
taking place.

'We liked going to their mosque and we liked sitting on the carpets and we liked the designs and the washing place was interesting.' (Genevieve, Holy Trinity)

'If we don't do this, they'd only know about Muslims and we'd only know about Christians and we'd start arguments.' (Jordan, Holy Trinity)

The return visit was to Holy Trinity Church followed by a picnic in the nearby park. Most of the Muslim children and some of their staff and parents had not been inside a church before. They enjoyed roaming freely around the building in pairs with our children to complete a church trail, and they asked many searching questions of the vicar. (A copy of the trail was sent to the Gatton teacher beforehand to make sure there weren't any inappropriate questions.) The picnic was good fun, though it's true to say that we all, children and staff alike, have to make an effort to talk with and play with 'the stranger' and not just sit with our familiar friends. Plenty of the children did mix in and were eager for the next exchange.

'I liked showing them round our church. I liked my partner.' (Shanelle, Holy Trinity)

'Walking to church with Aisha was nice, we found we both like laughing a lot.' (Tiya, Holy Trinity)

'I liked the bit when we had to answer the questions in the church.' (Abdul-Hakim, Gatton)

'It was very fun and I learned a lot. But they have names which are hard to remember.' (Rebecca, Holy Trinity)

'They are fun to play with. Kind, friendly and funny.' (Jazmin, Holy Trinity)

'No problems – but maybe we could decrease their volume!' (Ruqayyah, Gatton)

'Can we go for the whole day next time?' said lots of our children.

We have had our first 'friendly' football match and we are eagerly awaiting an invitation to swim in their swimming pool,

just completed, in their basement. Girls and boys will swim separately. On one visit the Gatton children were treated to a year
6 assembly with a memorably gruesome potted performance
of Shakespeare's *Macbeth*. Our staff members were invited to
Gatton's end-of-term staff rooftop barbeque, which was very
enjoyable, and a nice opportunity to meet without the children.

'When I went to the library, I saw three of the children from
Gatton. I went and talked to them. Fatima was one.' (Jimmy,
Holy Trinity)

SOS from Firdos: 'Sarah, can you come tomorrow? We've got a
delegation coming from the Ministry of Education to spend
the morning in the school. Please come and bear witness to our
exchange programme.'

'Firdos. Holy Trinity Church vicar has asked me to find a
Muslim, a Hindu, a Jew and a Buddhist to speak on different
evenings during Lent to a group of 40 or so Christians from his
congregation. Could you talk about 'The one-ness of God' and
what that means to you in your daily life? . . . Thank you.'

When Firdos and I first met in 2002 the controversy over single
faith schools was well stirred up, due to unrest in Oldham and
other northern towns which was attributed to social segregation
in some schools and communities.[3] This has not occurred in the
same way in South London because the religious minority communities are much more mixed in with the general population
(as can be seen in statistics, analysed by the Greater London
Authority,[4] from the 2001 national census). There are seven
Muslim schools in South London at the time of writing, of which
Gatton and one other are state funded and the others are private.
Almost all of the other single faith schools are Christian. Of
course, most of these Christian schools include children of other
faiths.

The debate rumbles on between those in favour and those
opposed to single faith schools. Arguments against: that they are
elitist, divisive and cause social segregation and are likely to
exacerbate racial and religious ignorance and intolerance.
Arguments in favour: that the spiritual and moral ethos of faith
schools is something to be valued and preserved; that parental
choice should be respected; that private single faith schools are

more likely to be 'ghettoised', introspective and bigoted than accountable state-supported schools.

Our future plans include staff joining up for some in-service training and collaborating on a teacher-training scheme, where trainee teachers will do a term's placement in our school and a term at Gatton School, and we're thinking about a joint parents' evening. However, Firdos has just left Gatton School, so here is the crunch. How much has this experiment been dependent on the enthusiasm of the two of us? Will the next head teacher of Gatton be keen to continue the exchanges? I (as a part-time teacher without class responsibilities) pay tribute to the year 5 teachers and support staff in both schools who have so willingly entered into the project, but there's always pressure on the timetable to fit in additional things. It has always been fun and appreciated once it happens, but it does require that extra effort to make it happen. And you need to believe in the benefits to make that effort. Will it continue?

Let me finish with part of a letter to Holy Trinity parents.

Why do we have our exchanges? Not primarily for religious education, although of course we do learn about each other's religious beliefs and practices. It's a wonderful opportunity for us (children, staff and parents) to get to know each other! An opportunity to talk with Muslims, to learn with and from them, to visit their mosque and to welcome them into our school and our church. An opportunity as Christians and Muslims, people of faith in God, to cross boundaries of 'difference' and relate as fellow human beings.

This is especially important in these times of stereotyping and suspicion stirred up by the media in response to national and international events which are way beyond our control. We must not allow these big outside issues to bring misunderstanding and strife into our local communities. Holy Trinity staff see links with Gatton as a contribution to peace and harmony with our neighbours and to the government's agenda of 'social cohesion'. Single faith schools are a controversial issue. One of the criticisms is that children should not grow up separately. So it seems like good practice to develop links between faith schools. Let's be pioneers of a positive way forward!

Note: Quotes in this chapter are from conversations with pupils and staff or from occasional questionnaires they have completed. (Spellings have been corrected.)

Response from Firdos Qazi, head teacher of Gatton School

Single faith schooling is a hot topic and one on which many people hold strong views. The viewpoints are clear but on what they are based is less easy to determine. It is clearly an emotive topic and currently also a very political one. At the ground level, though, it is just a matter of pragmatism. Many parents want their children to have an understanding of their faith and to spend their school days in an ethos where their faith values are evident.

Despite the fact that many people have moved away from religion altogether, some people cling to their faith. In times of difficulty, faith can give us something to hold fast to and it can be a comfort to know that there is a greater being who is aware of and concerned for our state.

People often say to me that religion is a divisive force. They state that it is the root cause of many an issue and so it must be bad: therefore, reducing the impact of religion will reduce the unrest between communities. I'm afraid I cannot see the logic of this at all. There will always be issues, people will always argue. Wars are over power, resources and pride, but it is harder to see these as 'moral grounds'. To me religion is a binding force – a force for good, a force for togetherness and unity. And when it is not, it is because we have misused our religion. We are all His creatures and it is to His power that we should bow.

Enough therefore of my own rantings. What does this all mean for my school? What has this to do with our partnership? Please let me explain.

Like Sarah, rather than argue for or against single faith schooling, I think we need to focus on the reality and any identified difficulties with this model. As with any type of 'segregation' or model of schooling which is selective (this can be based on ability as in grammar schools, on gender as in single sex schools, on ability to pay as in independent schools, or on faith), an unnatural divide is created. Certain pupils are pulled together and others excluded. As a result, issues arise. There are, however, in terms of education, a number of benefits. Where the benefits outweigh the drawbacks, it is only right to adopt the model. The real problems arise when, once having selected the way forward, we do nothing to mitigate the negative aspects.

Where our work has been exceptionally helpful is that it shows how the down-sides can be addressed creatively. With positive understanding and determination, with only minimal resources, pupils from two different faiths can share so much. It is really the will that is required, and possibly a model that thinks 'out of the box'. With these two ingredients, communities can help themselves.

I am incredibly indebted to Sarah for the dedication and skill with which she has collated and reported our experiences so effectively. I am convinced that, by sharing our little experiment, a seed will have been sown which will inspire other schools to make links and to develop what we have found to be an enriching experience.

Go, go, go – the sky is the limit. We can do it if it matters to us enough – and I know it does to enough people to make a difference.

Further reading

Bradford project: www.schoolslinkingproject.org.
Sarah Thorley, 2004, *Talking Together: Conversations about religion*, Ropley: John Hunt Publisher.
www.diversityanddialogue.org.uk.
www.schoolslinkingnetwork.org.uk.

Notes

1 *The Koran*, 1974, translated by N. J. Dawood, fourth revised edition, Harmondsworth: Penguin, p. 158.

2 At the time of writing, single faith schools are not legally obliged to teach their 'Locally Agreed Syllabus' (LAS) for Religious Education (as community schools must). Most LASs now include the teaching of all the major religions, throughout primary and secondary education. The (non-statutory) National Framework for RE, issued in 2004 by the then DfES, advocates this approach; it was officially endorsed by church and other faith leaders in 2006, as guidelines to be followed in single faith schools. But in practice, implementation varies greatly from one single faith school to another. (See also SACRE in Glossary.)

3 Siriol Davies, 2006, *An Evaluation of Different Models of Inter Faith Activity*, London: South London Inter Faith Group: available from South London Inter Faith Group, 24 Homewood Gardens, London SW2 3RS.

4 GLA (Greater London Authority). Religious Diversity Indices 2005.

3 Starting Out Together

The Greenwich Peninsula experience

MALCOLM TORRY

with responses by Ali Hassan Barakat and Harbhajan Singh

Then an angel showed me the river of the water of life, bright
as crystal, flowing from the throne of God and of the Lamb
through the middle of the street of the city. On either side of
the river is the tree of life with its twelve kinds of fruit, pro-
ducing its fruit each month; and the leaves of the tree are for
the healing of the nations.

Revelation 22.1–2

The circumference of the city shall be eighteen thousand
cubits. And the name of the city from that time on shall be, The
Lord is There.

Ezekiel 48.35

In February 2007 the construction site under the Millennium
Dome (now The O2) was reaching the peak of its activity. The
structure of the central 20,000-seat sports and music arena was
complete, and the buildings around it were nearly finished. On
Friday 9 February, workers on the site, who had received their
wages the day before, headed at break-time for one of the two
canteens for tea, sandwiches, or a full English breakfast – to
be met by display boards, a Salvation Army officer, a turban-
wearing Sikh, a Muslim imam, and a variety of Christian clergy.
It was the Greenwich Peninsula Chaplaincy's charity collection
day. We were collecting for Advocacy for Older People in
Greenwich, and for Salvation Army holidays for underprivileged
children and children at risk. We raised nearly £400 – a sum then
matched by the construction company, Sir Robert McAlpine.

The Millennium Year

The Greenwich Peninsula Chaplaincy isn't the first chaplains' team to operate in The O2. During 2000, at the Millennium Exhibition in the Dome, a team of 20 chaplains managed the Prayer Space and provided a chaplaincy service to both staff and visitors. The context was different, of course. The 2000 exhibition was an event to celebrate the 2,000th anniversary of Jesus' birth, so some aspects were specifically Christian: the panels and films at the heart of the Faith Zone were about the Christian faith, and the chaplains were Christian and led Christian prayers in the Prayer Space. There were several multi faith aspects to the event: people of all faiths were welcome to use the Prayer Space, festivals of all the faiths were celebrated in it, and the Faith Zone represented the ways in which a variety of faiths celebrate birth, marriage, death, and other life events. So one morning the Prayer Space was full of flowers ready for a Baha'i festival; during the morning chaplains, staff and visitors gathered for Christian prayers; and during the prayers a Buddhist came into the space to meditate. The book on the desk by the door was for anyone, of any faith, to record prayers.

Churches Together in England organised the chaplains' team: and we had Church of England, Free Church, Roman Catholic, Black Pentecostal and London City Mission chaplains. Each morning and afternoon two of us were on site. Some spent time in the Prayer Space; some wandered the Dome; and some, the author included, preferred the Diner: one of the canteens in which the 2007 charity collection day took place.

Relationships with the imam who visited the Dome were good, and Muslims furnished their own small mosque outside the Dome because the Dome had been paid for by the National Lottery and thus by the proceeds of gambling. (More on gambling later.)

In 2000 we were Christian chaplains. In 2007 we were Muslim, Sikh and Christian. The world has changed.

Planning together

At the end of 2000 the Dome closed. Proposals for the Dome came and went, until in 2002 Meridian Delta Ltd was appointed to develop the northern end of the Greenwich Peninsula on the basis of providing 10,000 dwellings, enough office space to fill two and a half Canary Wharf Towers, schools, a college and, in the Dome (now called The O2), an arena and entertainment district. It is in this new context that the different faith communities have started out together, have worked together, and have remained very different from each other.

The Borough of Greenwich contains two Sikh Gurdwaras, three Hindu Temples, a Mosque and a Mosque and Islamic Centre, a Baha'i community, a Buddhist Temple, a Quaker Meeting, and all sorts of churches, from numerous small black-led Pentecostal Churches meeting in people's homes to the huge New Wine Church in a refurbished cinema in Woolwich, from Free Churches and Church of England churches without a candle in sight to the Parish Church of St Nicholas, Plumstead, with its growing family of statues, and from mission halls and fellowships to a Roman Catholic Church with a grotto in the basement.

For 15 years the Greenwich Multi-Faith Forum has enabled volunteer representatives from the different faiths to meet each other, to organise multi faith walks (visiting different worship centres), to hold social events, and to be a focus for consultation of the faith communities, which plays an increasing role in the activity that the Government requires of local authorities. For even longer the Christian denominations have appointed Ecumenical Borough Deans. The Church of England, the Roman Catholic Church, the Baptist Church, independent free churches, black-led Pentecostal churches and the Salvation Army each have a Borough Dean, and the Methodist and United Reformed Churches share one. They meet, discuss issues of mutual concern, and represent the churches to the local authority.

So when in 2003 Susie Wilson of Meridian Delta Ltd, Steve Pallett of the London Borough of Greenwich, and myself as Team Rector of the Parish of East Greenwich convened a meeting to discuss how the faith communities were to involve themselves in the new community on the Greenwich Peninsula, the obvious recipients of invitations were members of the Greenwich Multi-Faith Forum and the Ecumenical Borough Deans.

The meeting agreed that the faith communities would work together on the Greenwich Peninsula; that together we would provide chaplaincy services to the different parts of the diverse community that would evolve there (construction workers, employers, employees, visitors, residents and students); that together we would manage and use a building for worship (separately), and for education, social activity, dialogue and community development (together); and that we would manage all of this activity together. We also agreed that there would be one point of contact between MDL, the borough and the faith communities, and the meeting appointed me to that task.

Was all of this agreed because there was no room in the masterplan for a number of separate religious buildings? Because the borough didn't want to relate to the different churches and the different faith communities separately in relation to buildings and activity? Because MDL didn't want to deal with lots of different committees, ministers and religious groups? Because in a multi faith society it is best for the faith communities to do together those things that they don't have to do separately? Because by working together we gain a deeper understanding of our own faith as well as a deeper understanding of other people's faiths? Because it's cheaper for all of us if we share a building, especially when we can't be sure what size congregations we'll be able to gather in a new community that is bound to contain a high proportion of mobile residents? And have we continued to do all of this together because the Community Development Foundation offers grants to organisations creating multi faith activity? Yes, for all these reasons, and probably for many others too. There's nothing wrong with mixed motives.

The 2003 meeting appointed a steering group called the Greenwich Peninsula Chaplaincy Steering Group, which became a registered charity, and has met regularly in order to appoint a team of chaplains, to review their work, and to plan for the future. The Steering Group has been multi faith from the beginning, and at the time of writing has Muslim, Sikh, Baha'i, Jewish, Christian and agnostic members.

Working together

Our first chaplains' team of three was rather the opposite of multi faith: two Church of England clergy and one Free Church minister. It's what we could get together when the O2 construction site opened in April 2005. At first there were only a few dozen workers, and a chaplain visiting the site a few days a week for an hour or so was all that was required; and, in any case, the appointment of a multi faith team to serve the site had hit a bit of a snag. Questions were being asked about whether it was possi-

ble to appoint Muslim and Sikh *chaplains*, based on the premise
that chaplaincy is a Christian concept – and rather an Anglican
one at that.

In prisons, universities, hospitals, industry, schools and other
institutions, a chaplain serves the spiritual and various other
needs of people regardless of whether they share the faith or
religious practice of the chaplain. Sometimes chaplains might
have a specific remit to serve the needs of people who identify
themselves with a particular faith (so a Hindu chaplain will serve
the religious needs of Hindus); but they might also have wider
responsibilities, and in a team of chaplains responsibilities might
be shared. (Hospital chaplains might have responsibility for particular wards, regardless of the faith commitments of the people
in them; and if so, they will refer individual patients to a chaplain
of their own faith as necessary.) In some contexts the chaplain
will draw no boundaries at all, as in industrial chaplaincy. I am
chaplain to the food refinery on the Greenwich Peninsula, and
my conversations are with everyone about everything.

The Church of England's parish system gives the parish priest
responsibilities for a geographical area and among the whole of
its population, not just in a congregation. It is this attitude that is
the basis of chaplaincy. In this country (but not necessarily in
countries where other faiths are in the majority) other faiths func-
tion differently: the role of an imam, a Hindu priest, a Sikh priest,
a Buddhist teacher or a rabbi is focused within the congregation,
in leading its worship and in teaching the faith's doctrine and its
implications, and in this context care of and attention to people of
different faiths or of none will often be a long way down the
agenda. One of the reasons for the faith leader concentrating
on the gathered congregation is that people who come to the
mosque, mandir, gurdwara, synagogue or temple come from a
wide area and don't identify with a geographical community in
the way people who attend an Anglican parish church might do;
and one of the reasons for this is the need for people of a minority
faith to maintain their identity. But whatever the basic differences, the Church of England's pastoral concern for everyone
living in a geographical parish fits nicely with the idea of chaplaincy, whereas the service of the religious needs of a gathered
congregation (of whatever faith) doesn't. Hence, in the UK, the
concern among some that chaplaincy might be a purely Christian
concept, and the argument that it is cultural imperialism for
Christians to attempt to involve other faiths in chaplaincy work.

But the argument in our context wasn't all in one direction, and there were some among the Islamic, Sikh and Hindu communities who were acquainted with chaplaincy in hospitals, hospices and prisons. For them, chaplaincy activity was potentially a means of serving a whole community and not merely their own co-religionists. So when the Steering Group advertised for volunteer chaplains for the construction site through the Greenwich Multi-Faith Forum, the Ecumenical Borough Deans, and the Steering Group's own Council of Reference (a group of faith community leaders set up to ensure good communications between the Steering Group and the wider faith communities), we received five applications: one from a Sikh, one from a Muslim, and three from Christians – a Salvation Army officer, a black Pentecostal pastor, and a retired Anglican priest. We shortlisted all of them, interviewed all of them, and appointed all of them. We trained them and took them to Bluewater near Dartford (mainly shops and restaurants) to experience the team of volunteer chaplains there (at Bluewater it's a Christian team). We got them all through the construction industry's health and safety training, and we set to work – and now we had enough volunteer chaplains to enable us to be present on the construction site for a couple of hours every weekday. And just in time, for the beginning of 2006 saw the number of construction workers rising rapidly. At its peak there were two thousand workers on the site, from almost every nationality, with a diversity of cultures and religions to match.

On a construction site a chaplain's task is to be available: in the canteens, in the offices, around the site. Availability leads to conversation: about the site, work, colleagues, employers, families, homesickness, ethics, religion, death, money ... One of the chaplaincy team's responsibilities was to maintain confidentiality, and another was to bring to management's attention things they ought to be aware of – such as racism, and mistreatment of one group of workers by another. By gathering up workers' concerns, communicating them, and not divulging who said what, a chaplain can both maintain confidentiality and communicate: a process which sometimes leads to change.

That makes it sound easy, but it isn't, of course. A canteen full of construction workers is not a comfortable situation for a chaplain. There is a natural tendency to sit with someone you've met before – but it might be someone else who wants to talk (though when you sit next to him he might not); or a different group which wants to raise an issue (or they might simply want to see if you'll collude with their racist prejudices). Wandering the site is no easier. Sometimes everyone is frantically busy. Sometimes they're not, and they clearly don't want to talk to a chaplain. Then someone stops you and tells you they're homesick; or about an issue on the site they don't know what to do about; or that their daughter is getting married and they're thrilled and want to tell someone who'll understand; or someone wants to tell you about a bereavement. Sometimes everyone sitting in the sun outside the canteen has their head in their newspaper or they're engrossed in a card game; but sometimes a discussion will turn into a deep learning experience – for the chaplain too. An engineer tells you how difficult it is to build a huge arena inside a big tent, where cranes can't be used; or a project planner tells you things are a bit behind but that they'll catch up. They might say that only a miracle will get something done on time, or that the chaplain had better tell God up there what's needed. The suggestion is half meant.

In July 2007 the construction site closed and The O2 opened for business. All the existing chaplains had expressed a willingness to stay in order to serve people working in The O2; and by the same method as before we recruited three more, another Sikh and two more Christians. We have trained the new chaplains and retrained ourselves (another trip to Bluewater), and with much assistance from the staff of Anschutz Entertainment Group, the proprietor of The O2, and from the managements of the different venues in The O2, we have set to work in the restaurants, cafés and bars in the entertainment district around the arena. It's all a bit different from a construction site, but our purpose is the same: availability, careful listening and confidentiality. If asked, a chaplain will share his or her faith, but not otherwise; and if necessary general concerns are communicated to management (but without mentioning names). Maybe one day we'll hold another charity collection.

Looking forward together

The next steps? A temporary building is promised from which we can serve the Peninsula's visitors, employees and residents, and eventually the Greenwich Pavilion (the glass and green steel building currently on the end of the Peninsula) will be moved south of The O2 to provide us with more space for these tasks. How using these buildings together will work out we don't know, but what we do know is that we've planned the temporary building together (particularly in relation to ablution facilities for those faith communities for whom washing before worship is important), and that the Steering Group will be in charge. We also know already how the worship of the different faith communities will be timetabled. Muslim Friday prayers will be at lunchtime on Fridays; Christian congregations will meet on Sundays (and Saturday evenings for Roman Catholics); and Sikh and Hindu worship might occur on Sunday afternoons or maybe Saturdays. There are almost no Jews in Greenwich, but that doesn't mean that there won't be any in the new community on the Peninsula, and Friday evening might see Jews worshipping in the temporary building and then the Pavilion. There are the Buddhists, and the Baha'is (who have a counter-cultural nineteen-day cycle), and possibly even Jains and Zoroastrians. Then there are the festivals of the different traditions to fit in.

One of the presuppositions with which we are working is that we shall be doing together everything that we can in good conscience do together (such as workplace chaplaincy), and separately everything else (such as prayer and worship). But there is a variety of Christian denominations, each with its own worship tradition. For some denominations worship cannot be shared: for Roman Catholics, the Mass is an obligation, a Roman Catholic priest must preside, and the form of worship must be of the authorised kind. With other denominations there are two options: holding a variety of acts of worship jointly planned and led, or holding a variety of acts of worship, each one planned and led by a different denomination. I suspect that we shall see both patterns. We shall see some acts of worship planned and led by single denominations simply because that's easier to manage and because it makes accountability clear. We shall also see some acts of worship jointly planned and led – which will add to the variety of kinds of Christian worship. Inevitably, the worship timetable will look as if it's predominantly Christian; and generally, because the chaplains' team is already predominantly Christian, religious activity on the Peninsula could easily appear to be basically Christian, with other faith communities contributing.

I don't see what we can do about this. The Christian faith is still numerically stronger than the other faiths (and certainly this is the case in Greenwich); there are more paid and non-stipendiary

authorised Christian ministers than there are authorised ministers of other faith communities; the churches have the kinds of
structures that enable them more easily to appoint trustees and
to recommend volunteer chaplains; and the Church of England
in particular, and the Roman Catholic and Free Churches to some
extent, have long-standing and deep community links which
enable relationships with secular organisations to emerge and
develop. This means that mainstream Christian churches, and
the Church of England in particular, are more likely to be insti-
gators and drivers of such projects as the Greenwich Peninsula
Chaplaincy – which makes it more important than ever that
everyone involved in such projects, and particularly Christians,
and particularly members of the Church of England, should do
all they can to develop areas of genuine equality between the
faith communities, both in theory and in practice.

Learning together

One of the first activities of the Steering Group was to educate
itself about the options for working in a multi faith way. To this
end we visited the Canary Wharf Prayer Room and an inter faith
centre in West Kilburn.

When the Canary Wharf development was planned the
churches (and particularly one of the Church of England parishes on the Isle of Dogs) took an entirely negative attitude to it.
Many in the local community weren't happy about the plans,
and the church took a leading role as the community expressed
its anger. The office blocks went up anyway. Maybe if the church
had kept open channels of communication between the community and the developer the outcome for future relationships and
for the way the development happened might have been somewhat different. One of the outcomes of improved relationships is
a Prayer Room, and another is the Bishop of London's appointment of a chaplain to Canary Wharf. The chaplaincy is Christian,
but the Prayer Room has a multi faith management committee
and is used by a variety of faith communities. This is the 'level
playing field' model of multi faith work.

In West Kilburn two Christian churches (Church of England
and United Reformed Church) built new premises together and
invited a variety of faith communities to use them. This is the
'host and visitor' model.

We chose the level playing field model. All that I have written above about the Christian faith being better represented than the other faiths remains true, but the *structure* of the Greenwich Peninsula Chaplaincy is multi faith, and structurally there is a level playing field. At the moment the Chair of the Steering Group is an Evangelical Free Church pastor, but could be a Baha'i. The site chaplain is a Christian, but could be a Muslim or a Sikh. The paid staff member is a Christian, but could be a Hindu, a Buddhist, a Jain, an agnostic or an atheist. (There is no occupational requirement that the postholder should have a personal faith. What is required is an ability to work with the chaplaincy's aims and objectives.[1])

As well as visiting others' projects in order to educate ourselves, we have also held consultation events to enable the borough's faith communities to participate in the chaplaincy's planning for the future. Two of these events have been presentations of progress to a gathering of people who had responded to invitations offered through the Greenwich Multi-Faith Forum, the Ecumenical Borough Deans, and the Council of Reference. Questions and discussion followed, and then workshops on particular aspects of the chaplaincy's current and future work. Another event was a visit of the four Presidents of Churches Together in England in 2004 (the Archbishop of Canterbury, the Archbishop of Westminster, the Moderator of the Free Churches Group, and a representative of the Black Majority Churches). Yes: again, this was a Christian visit – but next time it might be the Muslim Council of Great Britain, or the Chief Rabbi, asking to visit the chaplaincy.

A particularly important consultation exercise was a longer and deeper one, on how the chaplaincy should react to the possibility of a Regional Casino in The O2. Members of the Steering Group, chaplains, members of the Council of Reference and others were consulted on their faiths' attitudes to gambling. They prepared a paper which was issued in July 2005 as the Greenwich Peninsula Chaplaincy's position paper. The story of the controversy surrounding a document published on the Government's Casino Advisory Panel's website and purporting to represent the chaplaincy's views has been told elsewhere.[2] What is relevant here is the fact that early consultations between the faith communities meant that we were ready for the debate, and for the Casino Advisory Panel's decision on where the one Regional Casino was to be located. So on the day of the announcement we had two press releases ready: one if the decision was for Greenwich, and one if it was for elsewhere. It was the latter that we needed.

One of the important lessons we've learnt is that healthy multi faith activity requires thorough and wide-ranging consultation. We have learnt that it needs good planning (whenever a temporary building appears we'll be ready for it); and it needs flexibility, for working among the Peninsula's residents and office workers will be very different from working on a construction site or in an entertainment district, and the ways in which the different faith communities collaborate with each other will be different. In the residential community the different faith communities will need to operate both together and separately, and this will present us with some new challenges. We have learnt that doing things together requires clear governance structures and clarity about what we're doing together and what we're doing separately, but above all we've learnt that, if faith communities are going to work together in a new community, the first essential is starting out together.

This book is about Christians working with other faiths, so a final word to the Christian Church is relevant. On the Greenwich Peninsula the denominational structures of the churches active in the area have shown considerable understanding of the chaplaincy's multi faith approach, and have actively supported it. Representatives of the leaderships of the Roman Catholic and Anglican Churches are co-chairs of the Council of Reference; and the Bishop of Woolwich (for the Church of England) and the Auxiliary Bishop of the Archdiocese of Southwark (for the Roman Catholic Church) have both shown particular interest in the project and have visited Steering Group meetings and The O2. The Church of England has taken a leading role in the sense that the local team rector is the site chaplain; and at the same time it has supported the 'level playing field' approach and the plan for multi faith buildings, which means that Church of England congregations will be using shared space rather than having a building of their own.

While no faith communities active on the Peninsula have sizeable human or financial resources, the Church of England as a whole has more than any other. It therefore has two responsibilities: to make them available in support of the multi faith project; and not to attempt to dominate the project, either structurally or in practice. In this case the Diocese of Southwark and its representatives have behaved impeccably, and have understood well the tensions I experience as team rector of a Church of England parish with responsibility to an independent charitable trust for the activities of a multi faith chaplaincy team operating within the parish boundaries.

Above all, a project such as this requires clarity about what is to be done together and what is to be done separately. There will be separate Christian denominational congregations and activities, *and* there will be Christians of different denominations worshipping together; *and* there will be chaplaincy, community development, social and educational activity undertaken together with all the faith communities represented on the Peninsula. The different faiths will quite legitimately want to conduct their own missions among the different parts of the evolving Peninsula community. They will also continue to look for activities that can be carried out together. In a few years' time perhaps there will be another book and I'll be able to tell how we've got on on the other construction sites that will open soon and in the new residential areas, office blocks and other institutions soon to arrive.

The Greenwich Peninsula will in many ways be a microcosm – literally a 'small world': a diverse, multiethnic, multicultural and multi faith world. How we manage to work together and differently in this small world will have some important things to say about how the different faiths will work together and differently on larger canvases.

Response by Sheikh Ali Hassan Barakat

This chapter highlights the new challenges facing chaplaincy work in Britain in general, and in Greenwich in particular. After all, we can no longer talk of a uniform society in Greenwich, but only about a multicultural and multi faith one. This has a considerable impact on chaplaincy work, triggering the need for it to change, often in a revolutionary way, rapidly, and according to need and possibility. It now requires the chaplain to be aware not only of the needs of the people who share the same faith, but also of the needs of everyone in the community, whatever their faith and background.

As a Muslim chaplain, I have really been humbled to be part of the chaplaincy team on the Greenwich Peninsula. I think that the multi faith approach is everything a multi faith community needs, and I think it will contribute considerably to the way we live together in Greenwich.

To create a chaplaincy team made up of members of a variety of faiths was a wise move. With such a diverse and multicultural community in the Greenwich Peninsula, we need to hear the voices of the different people that make it up. This is the only way we can tackle misunderstandings, and promote equal opportunities and fair treatment for all.

Moreover, working in the chaplaincy team has enabled me to learn about the different faiths of some of my colleagues. In the time we have been working together to serve the community as spiritual leaders and in other ways, we have all gained something for ourselves: a greater understanding of one another's religions – our differences and also our similarities. Particularly in the case of the casino debate we have discovered our similarities of outlook. When this issue came to us, we were united by a common belief in the importance of families and by our determination not to let the safety and integrity of our existing communities disintegrate: not after so much has gone into making it the way it is, and the long bridge of effort and hopes which we are currently working on to make it better.

Response by Harbhajan Singh

This chapter rightly asks whether the Church of England has too much control over the chaplaincy project. It is certainly true that the project is totally controlled and managed by middle-class Church of England vicars. What matters most is whether they are competent, committed, and professionally trained to lead such a project. No eyebrows should go up if a Sikh or a Muslim member of the chaplaincy is one day given the responsibility to lead such a project, as long as that individual is qualified and competent to do such a job. This positive thinking will lead to more understanding among diverse faith communities and will then help towards community cohesion. Community cohesion cannot happen in isolation and by waving a magic wand. Long term it must be based on equality, sincerity and justice. Those groups less powerful will be frustrated if, due to a lack of capacity-building initiatives and schemes, they don't get training and skills and are therefore not able to take a leading role. The Faith Community

Capacity Building funding currently on offer seems to have made a sterling start. I hope it continues. So far, it's only a beginning, but you have to start somewhere.

And now for a most significant event during our time as chaplains on the construction site: the Greenwich Peninsula Chaplaincy charity collection day. It was like a dream come true. At my suggestion, Advocacy for Older People in Greenwich was selected as one of the two charities to be supported by the Greenwich Peninsula Chaplaincy. The end product of the charity day was wonderful: £400 collected in six hours' hard work by the members of a dedicated team. It also gelled the team together.

I'm not sure how our chaplaincy role will change now that The O2 is up and running. But I'm totally convinced that our involvement with local schools, shops, and hundreds and thousands of people coming to enjoy the Greenwich Peninsula – and particularly the vast number of families moving into newly built homes – is the challenge that attracted me to the Greenwich Peninsula Chaplaincy team. People have sometimes been confused and baffled at how a Sikh could be a chaplain. Many a time I've had the feeling that a person in the Diner doesn't want to speak to me, and at the same time I've been convinced that he has got something to share with me. This has given me even more strength and inspiration to engage him in a meaningful dialogue, which has often ended up as a good heart-to-heart chat for fifteen to twenty minutes. There have been many such successful encounters which have really encouraged me to go to the construction site every Monday, sometimes with a broken umbrella and being blown away by a gust of wind and heavy rain. This reminds me of John Wesley, the famous Methodist travelling preacher, and of Guru Nanak, founder of the Sikh faith, on his long and hard world travels. My trips around The O2 construction site were only a miniature in comparison. I enjoyed every second of it, and I am enjoying The O2 itself now that it is open. I would urge everybody who has compassion and a mind to help their fellow brothers and sisters to become part of a chaplaincy, whether in a hospital, a prison or a shopping centre.

Further reading

Anschutz Entertainment Group Ltd.: www.aegworldwide.com.
The Borough of Greenwich: www.greenwich.gov.uk.
English Partnerships: www.englishpartnerships.co.uk.

The Government's Casino Advisory Panel: www.culture.gov.uk/cap/.

The Greenwich Multi Faith Forum: www.gmff.uk.com.

The Greenwich Peninsula Chaplaincy: www.greenwich-peninsula-chaplaincy.org.uk.

Meridian Delta Ltd: www.meridiandeltaltd.com.

The O2: www.theo2.co.uk.

Malcolm Torry (ed.), 2004, *The Parish: People, Place and Ministry: A Theological and Practical Exploration*, Norwich: Canterbury Press.

Malcolm Torry (ed.), 2006, *Diverse Gifts: Varieties of lay and ordained ministries in the Church and community*, Norwich: Canterbury Press.

Notes

1 (1) To advance religion by serving the religious, pastoral, educational and social needs of the public working in, frequenting, visiting or residing in the Greenwich Peninsula and the neighbouring area; (2) to promote religious harmony and understanding by raising awareness of the different religious traditions; (3) to promote any other charitable purposes that the trustees from time to time determine.

2 Malcolm Torry (ed.), 2007, *Regeneration and Renewal: The Church in new and changing communities*, Norwich: Canterbury Press, ch. 11. The chaplaincy's position paper can be found at the end of that chapter, and also at www.greenwich-peninsular-chaplaincy.org.uk/newsletter.html.

4 Facing Challenges Together

The Clapham and Stockwell Faith Forum responding to world events

CATRIONA ROBERTSON

with a response by James Baaden

What does the Lord require of you but to do justice, and to love kindness, and to walk humbly with your God?

Micah 6.8

We have created you from a male and a female and divided you into nations and tribes that you might get to know one another.

The Holy Qur'an, Sura 49.13[1]

It's hard to think back to how things were at the beginning of July 2005, just before the London bombs. In Stockwell, I was involved with the local Faith Forum, preparing for a community fun-day.

Clapham and Stockwell Faith Forum is a local multi and inter faith group. Our management committee currently includes Anglican clergy and laity, Sunni and Shi'a Muslims, people from the Jewish, Baha'i and Hindu traditions, and our local Methodist minister. We bring together people of all faiths and of none. We run women's groups, teenagers' football teams and structured round table discussions for 'hot' issues. We work in partnership with many local organisations, organise faith literacy training, and are often consulted by public sector bodies. We respond to local events and concerns – and we have had our fair share of these – but our overall ethos is enjoyment: we like getting together and sharing food, stories, hopes and reflections.

Peace, shalom, salaam, shanti

At the first Stockwell Festival in the summer of 2001, the Forum released dozens of white balloons into the sky with messages of peace. It was a gusty day and the balloon strings plaited themselves together in a trice. Deciding not to battle against the wind to untangle them any further, we released them all together and they shot up towards the scudding clouds. For our first contribution to public life, you could say it was a sign of things to come: the three founders of the Faith Forum, myself (an Anglican layperson), an Anglican clergyman, and the Chairman of the local mosque, were to get to know each other much better over the next few years (along with people from other faith traditions) and our lives, and those of our communities, would be woven together far more closely than before.

Each year at the Festival we provide a peace tent (a beautiful circular yurt) where local people of all ages can relax on the carpets, enjoy a cup of tea, browse through our books and resources, play co-operative games, and join in workshops and discussions. Local people from very different walks of life are tempted to kick off their shoes, explore what the peace tent has to offer, and relax. The special ambience and safe space that the yurt provides seems to allow different kinds of encounter and conversation. Some people pop in just to have a look and end up staying for hours. Children love it; babies often fall asleep.

The programme of activities promotes ways of tackling the inevitable difficulties of city life in positive and non-violent ways. We have offered introductions to mediation, anti-bullying strategies, anger management, the slow movement (not everything benefits from being done as fast as possible), counselling, relaxation methods, restorative justice, and baby massage. Sometimes we draw the lines of a small labyrinth with a trail of flour on the grass outside: labyrinths have had significance across different faith traditions for centuries. The approach is low-key and enjoyable. There is a lot of laughter. There is very little, if any, overtly religious content, and any faith-related material or discussion always involves more than one faith tradition.

One year we hosted the Forgiveness Project photo exhibition. It shows individuals from the opposite sides of violent conflicts who have worked hard to understand one another, and in many cases have found alternatives to revenge and discovered the empowering nature of forgiveness.

In 2005, the peace tent flyers had gone out for Saturday 9 July, a programme of activities was arranged, and I was attending to the last-minute details: liaising with one of the local primary schools and finding the right kind of chair for the head masseuse. We were working with the South London Inter Faith Group, which was planning to visit two of our member faith communities and the peace tent itself on the day of the Festival as part of its annual inter faith walk. Forum members were looking forward to a concert of music and recitation from different faith traditions at the South London Liberal Synagogue on the evening of 7 July. Inspired by an article about the Peace Mala in the *Connect* booklet published by the Inter Faith Network for the UK, we had contacted the Welsh charity and ordered forty of their Peace Mala wristbands. The Peace Mala is a symbolic bracelet that has been designed to promote friendship, respect and peace between the faiths, cutting through prejudice and celebrating what makes us different from each other. Each coloured bead on the band represents a different faith tradition and the Mala is worn to demonstrate that, although people have different religious beliefs, we work together for the common good. *Mala* is the word used by Hindus, Sikhs and Buddhists for prayer beads.

When news of the explosions started coming in on the morning of Thursday 7 July, my first concern was for my son's friends who were part of a young American lacrosse team on an exchange visit. They had gone sight-seeing and, with the mobile phone network down, it was some time before we were able to reassure their parents in the USA. Soon the reports started to suggest, first, that the explosions had been caused by bombs, and then that the bombers were likely to have claimed a link with the Muslim religion. Members of the Forum contacted each other by landline and email as soon as we could – were we OK, how were our communities responding, what could we, as a Faith Forum, do to help? We were all shocked by the violence, concerned for the victims and worried about possible knock-on effects, particularly on the Muslim community.

The obvious place for a united response was the peace tent. We discussed a joint statement – something which would defy the bombers' attempt to create divisions between us. Toaha Qureshi, Chairman of the local mosque and the Forum's treasurer and co-founder, Jasmine Read, the Forum's Secretary from the Baha'i faith, and I tried to put something together with which all local people from any faith community (or none) would be happy to align themselves. I suggested, 'No act of violence will break us apart.' Jasmine wanted something stronger, a word we could all relate to, rather than one from which we could distance ourselves by applying it only to others: 'No act of aggression will break us apart.' We agreed to start the statement with, 'Our multi-faith community flourishes. We celebrate our diversity.' This had been our experience together and we wanted to affirm it. We imagined how we might say this, together, in the peace tent. The ideal time would be when our friends from the South London Inter Faith Group arrived. Just saying something while standing around or sitting down did not seem satisfactory. I suggested holding hands in a circle to show our strength and solidarity with one another. 'No, no, we cannot have that,' Toaha pointed out. It would be impossible for most of his Muslim friends to join in – men joining hands with women is not always permitted and we didn't want to have two circles. I remembered the Peace Mala wristbands – what if we made a human peace mala? We could all hold on to something circular and make the statement together without having to hold hands. But what? A bit of string or ribbon seemed rather feeble.

Late on Friday afternoon I found the only ships' chandlers I know, on the river bank in Putney. I was looking for strong rope, the thickest they had, and preferably not in a fluorescent colour. I found some natural fibre rope, about an inch and a half in diameter – perfect. How could I stick it together to make a circle, I asked, knowing very little about rope, knots or anything to do with sailing. We can splice it together for you, they said. Within an hour I was heading back to Stockwell with a huge coil of off-white rope in the back of the car – soft to the touch but heavy and very strong. Continuing the Welsh Peace Mala image, I wondered about colours. Jasmine, Toaha, David (our Jewish committee member) and the other contributors to the peace tent event were happy with the rope and had no objection to adding colours. The local post office had some rainbow crepe paper – if we cut it up into its various colours, people would be able to choose one to represent their faith (or just their favourite colour) and add it to the 'mala' to represent our diverse religious traditions. As an impulse buy, I added a packet of luggage labels: after joining in the statement, people might want to write their own personal message of peace and tie it on to the rope peace mala. If I was feeling rather helpless in the face of scary events, others might be feeling that way too and might welcome the chance to do something positive, to express themselves.

On the day of the Festival, over sixty South London Inter Faith walkers, accompanied by Forum members from Stockwell Mosque and Stockwell Methodist Church, arrived at the peace tent. The peace mala rope already had some colours and a few messages attached. Local people joined in and we held the rope and made the statement of solidarity together. Even though the circle of the rope was wide, not everyone could hold it and I noticed some people touching the shoulder of the rope-holder in front, in order to be part of the symbolic act. I have a vivid memory of the range of people holding on to the peace mala rope – traditionally dressed Muslim men, someone with a Mohican haircut, teenagers, white-haired men, African Caribbean women and women wearing jeans, shalwar kameez and other weekend outfits. Some went on to say a few words, including a friend of the Forum from the Muslim community, Saleha Jaffer, who had been giving relaxing Indian head massage to visitors. At the end of the festival, the peace mala rope was taken to Stockwell Mosque. But within two weeks it was needed again.

The Stockwell shooting

Thursday 21 July 2005 brought four more attempted bombings in London, only this time the bombs did not explode. Police activity rose to an unprecedented level in order to find the perpetrators.

On the morning of Friday 22 July, the police shot a young man as he sat in a train at Stockwell tube station. At first we assumed that the police had found and killed one of the failed bombers. To many local people, particularly those who came from countries where police shootings are more common, this produced a feeling of unease.

Stockwell tube station was taped off. Heavily armed police kept guard and white-suited forensic investigators moved around. The world's media set up camp. The TV cameras and well-turned-out journalists created a further exclusion zone around what was, for us, our home territory. Traffic was not allowed through, adding a quiet eeriness. We wandered around, bumping into friends and neighbours, eager to talk, ask questions, and exchange bits of information.

Again the telephone and email lines were busy among Forum

members. Agreeing a form of words to express a clear view without ambiguity is time-consuming, but we managed a few sentences (see Appendix 1, page 49) which expressed condemnation of the bombings, support for the emergency services, and a statement of solidarity with the Mosque in working for a cohesive, peaceful and just society. This was read out at Friday prayers at the Mosque.

When it was announced the next day that the man who had been killed was not one of the bombers but was in fact an innocent man, we felt even more confused and concerned. Later in the day the police named the young man as Jean Charles de Menezes, a Brazilian, who had no connection with the attempted bombings that week. Until then, the mood locally (and throughout the capital) had been compared to the spirit of the Blitz – people pulling together, supporting the emergency services and helping one another through a difficult time – but this new piece of information threw many of us into a bewildering mix of fear and ignorance. With a very large Portuguese-speaking population in Stockwell, young men were immediately aware of being in a new situation. What had gone wrong? Would the police make another mistake? The Muslim community suspected that Jean Charles had been shot because he was mistaken for a Muslim. How should our young men protect themselves not only from suicide bombers, but also from police mistakes? It appeared that Jean Charles had done nothing to warrant being shot and had not even been able to explain who he was. Mothers, fathers, sisters, brothers, friends – the whole community immediately felt more vulnerable.

Toaha went up to Birmingham for a large Muslim conference. We discussed what more the Forum could do. The local police, who had not been involved in the shooting and were as shocked as any of us at the tragic death of an innocent man, called key people together to share the latest information, but it was clear that the borough police were only slightly better informed than the rest of us. After checking with other committee members, we decided on a local gathering – not a public meeting with microphones and speeches, but a chance to listen to each other and to reflect. Toaha said he wouldn't be able to make it down from Birmingham by Sunday evening, but we decided to go ahead all the same. The school holidays had just begun and by Monday morning people would have to be, somehow or other, getting on with their lives. Emails and text messages zipped about and the bush telegraph was busy. The community centre was packed when the allotted time came on Sunday.

All the Stockwell Mosque keyholders were with Toaha in Birmingham and we could not retrieve the peace mala rope. Nevertheless, we sat in concentric circles around a large table covered in colour, as if the mala were there, and we encouraged everyone to feel a sense of togetherness. We started with a period of shared silence. We read out the statement we had made on 9 July, but this time the 'act of aggression' that was uppermost in people's minds was the police shooting. There was an opportunity for people to talk to the person sitting next to them: what were they feeling, how were their families affected, what were their concerns? Back in the round, some shared their thoughts and fears. Some also made political speeches, but were held in check by others who felt this was too dark a time to be scoring points.

The Archdeacon of Lambeth, local Anglican and Methodist clergy, and the local Roman Catholic priest all helped us with their prepared reflections. The Archdeacon talked about the nature of anger, of fear: we had a choice about what we did with these strong emotions. The speakers also pointed to the power of faith and trust. Before the Borough Commander of Police spoke, Toaha appeared at the door with his colleagues: they had left Birmingham early and came straight to the community centre, wearing their white robes and hats. Toaha said how sad he felt about the death of an innocent man and offered his condolences to the family. He realised that the association being made between the acts of violence in London and his religion meant that he himself was being viewed with suspicion, especially when wearing his special clothes for worship. The Forum's gathering that evening of 24 July was the first of many public gatherings in the wake of the shooting of Jean Charles de Menezes.

Languages of peace, shared experience

Over the summer, the peace mala rope collected more colours and more messages of peace as it travelled to meetings at the Mosque, to an Anglican church open day on Brixton Hill, to community centres, and to the Peace Garden in Brixton, where the peace tent was pitched for the second time that year. In Brixton we were surrounded by traffic noise and sirens as well as several men who were unsteady on their feet with a beer can or an unusually long roll-up cigarette in their hands. Unaccompanied children made themselves at home and an amplified demonstration about deaths in police custody continued all afternoon. Creating a peaceful space was a challenge, but it worked, and the heartfelt conversations that took place that day, as well as the new messages attached to the peace mala rope, were humbling.

The messages are written in English, Portuguese, Spanish, Arabic, Hebrew and other languages. Some are simple and straightforward, some quote favourite thinkers, others seem to come straight from the heart and from difficult experiences.

The mala rope has been used to bring people from different faith traditions together symbolically at the Prayers for World Peace at Southwark Cathedral on Remembrance Sunday in 2005 and 2006. After these ceremonies, people read the luggage labels and, realising that the messages represent a mixed bag of pain, hope and encouragement, often add their own. At a Forum gathering at Stockwell Mosque in 2006 to discuss the publication of controversial cartoons about Islam in Danish newspapers, the presence of the mala (and the associations it now brings) helped us to remember our shared history. We have already been through some difficult times together – and we pulled through stronger.

The anniversary of the London bombing, 7 July, fell on a Friday in 2006, and we took the peace mala rope to Stockwell Mosque to hold the minute's silence at noon in commemoration of the victims of the bombs and their families. Forum members from a variety of Christian traditions and from the Jewish tradition, including women, were invited inside to join the men worshipping at Friday prayers. We were formally welcomed and offered refreshments afterwards. It was good to recognise some of the faces we had seen at Forum events in the past and to be greeted by so many worshippers. I remembered the first time I had knocked on the door of the Mosque five years earlier, when I had recognised no one. The backdrop of international and national events since then had also brought our local Muslim friends into sharper focus: each time Islam reached the headlines, the impact was felt in day-to-day life. We discovered that a local shop assistant was asked to remove his topi hat so that he didn't put customers off; women drivers wearing the hijab headscarf were less likely to be let into traffic from a side road. I was glad

Forum members were able to show our support for all the good work being done for local marginalised and unemployed young people by Stockwell Green Community Services, under the umbrella of the Mosque.

Exporting the peace, not importing the wars

Later that year, in November 2006, the peace mala rope (which by then had a well-worn look) was again in service. Intense Israeli military action in Beit Hanoun in Gaza had resulted in the violent deaths of civilians, mostly women and children. This was widely condemned in the press and formally regretted by the Israeli government itself. Rabbi James Baaden, on his way to a multi faith meeting at his own synagogue, found it plastered with huge press photographs of the dead casualties. There was no way of knowing who had affixed the images. Later that night, Rabbi Baaden sent an email to all on his regular list, including friends and colleagues of other faiths. Immediately, Forum members wanted to offer support to the Synagogue congregation and to express our condemnation of offensive, wrong-headed and anonymous desecration of a place of worship. If the people who carried out this carefully planned act had troubled to contact the Synagogue congregation, they would have discovered that South London synagogues are not outposts of the Israeli army.

Toaha was out of town again, this time in Pakistan. I managed to get through to his family by mobile phone. From Multan, Toaha gave his full support to a statement condemning the desecration and standing in solidarity with the Synagogue congregation. There was some discussion with other members of the Forum as to what constituted desecration, but after a very short exchange of emails and telephone calls it was decided that any place of worship should be fully respected, that a line had been crossed, and that we should release a statement. This was a new situation for us – places of worship are normally well respected in Lambeth.

We rang around Lambeth faith groups to ensure that our statement was something everyone could stand by. Christians were the most cautious: while some wanted simply to denounce the affixing of the photos to a place of worship and the implied complicity of the Synagogue in the deaths of the women and children, others preferred to 'balance' this with an equally strong denunciation of the military action that had led to the death of innocent civilians. Others were concerned that the Forum could be seen to be taking sides and were hesitant to ally themselves publicly with any action that could be misconstrued as supporting the Israeli government. An attempt to gather people of different faiths on the steps of the Synagogue failed. The final statement (see Appendix 2, page 49) was released and immediately endorsed by local and national figures in public life.

We all learned more about what it is like to be Jewish that weekend. Anti-Semitism remains a very sensitive subject for debate, even in multi faith circles. Strong views among some Christians on the plight of Palestinian people can obscure a clear view of local Jewish life. We learned that the Jewish community in South London had moved into its new synagogue during the same month in 1938 as *Kristallnacht*, the night when Nazi Germany was destroying Jewish businesses, homes and synagogues on a large scale and murdering German Jewish citizens. Many of us had not known about the long trail of anti-Jewish propaganda over the centuries which has involved images of child-killing. The photos of the children killed by the Israeli army in Gaza were terrible for all of us to see, but we didn't know about the deep resonance felt in the hearts of the Synagogue congregation until we were told.

I arranged to take the peace mala rope and the statement up to the Synagogue that Friday (Sabbath) evening. On my way, I called in on Sarah Thorley, a Lambeth resident and someone who has been at the forefront of inter faith activity in South London for many years. I was delighted when she agreed to come with me. Rabbi Baaden received the peace mala rope graciously, albeit with some curiosity, along with a copy of the statement and our assurance of support.

Religion School at the Synagogue takes place on Sunday mornings, and the children not only added their own messages of peace in English and Hebrew, but decorated the luggage labels with wonderful sequins, glitter and coloured drawings. When Rabbi Baaden brought the mala to Southwark Cathedral that evening for Inter Faith Prayers for World Peace on Remembrance Sunday, the mala had acquired a whole new series of messages. Later, the Synagogue's newsletter noted, 'it brought us comfort and made us feel we were not alone'.

The peace mala rope on the Common

Celebratory events also benefit from the mala: the Forum's 14-year-old multi faith football players (modestly named Lambeth FC) received their end of season medals on a windy day in April 2007 on Clapham Common. The multi faith aspect of the football club is not laboured, but each player was given a wristband Peace Mala from Wales and the rope version was laid on the grass to mark out a circle for speeches and medals. Its ordinariness as a circle of rope, its strength, and the curious luggage labels and colours all around seem to command respect. No one crossed into the centre of the circle unless invited to receive a prize, and every boy had at least one turn in the centre. Toaha Qureshi and a new member of the Forum's committee, the Revd Rob Hufton, the Minister of Clapham Methodist Church, gave out the prizes.

I recently placed another order with Pam Evans, the creator of the colourful Peace Mala wristbands, which many people are now wearing in South London. I learned that she has taken up the rope idea herself and is using it in her inter faith work in schools in Wales. Faith communities in Waltham Forest, after hearing about our peace mala rope in Stockwell, have used a circular rope during times of community tension. The ideas flow back and forth.

We have learned so much from the use of the mala. Although I, familiar with a western church way of doing things, place the peace mala rope on the floor, I've noticed that in the Mosque and in the Synagogue it is often moved, respectfully, on to a large table. Nothing is said, but I understand, and I have come to value the strong rope, which now represents so much of the Forum's life together.

Response by Rabbi James Baaden

Judaism situates holiness in the dimension of time rather than space. Time, and not the realm of buildings, places and things, is the key framework in which we encounter God. The Hebrew Bible specifies units of holy time – the Sabbath, the Festivals, life-cycle rituals, sacrifices, other divinely 'appointed moments' – and also puts the emphasis on the passage of time in other ways: through the narrative of creation and the generations of the

Patriarchs and Matriarchs in Genesis, or the story of slavery and liberation in Exodus, or the vision of the Prophets, who confronted the spirit of their age and interpreted the course of events. True, one fragment of the last version of ancient Judaism's one holy place, the Temple in Jerusalem, namely the Western Wall (sometimes called the 'Wailing Wall'), has survived to become an object of something like veneration. Nevertheless, in general, the Judaism of these past two millennia has been unfamiliar with shrines, holy places and altars. Synagogues aren't temples: the word 'synagogue' simply means 'meeting house'.

And yet. Catriona Robertson notes that she has observed Muslims and Jews lifting the peace mala rope off the floor and putting it on a table. I know that this was my instinct, certainly. In spite of what I write above, Judaism does know the concept of *klei kodesh*, 'objects of holiness' (literally 'utensils' or 'instruments'), and these do not belong on the floor. A good example would be a prayerbook. If one of these happens to end up on the floor, the traditional practice when retrieving it – commonplace in my Liberal synagogue as it would be in an Orthodox one – is to kiss it. To my mind, this is more an expression of love than of reverence. The scrolls of the Torah (Pentateuch) are thought of as objects of religious reverence, to be sure, but it occurs to me that the emotion with which they are treated is in fact love: they are wrapped in beautiful fabrics, decorated with jewels, carried in our arms, and gently taken from and returned to the ark.

And so the peace mala rope inspired love immediately when it appeared in our community. It came to us in a time of grief and bitterness. The huge laminated photographs of dead Palestinian children will never leave my memory. There they were, stuck to the doors of the synagogue as I arrived to set things up, as it happened, for an inter faith meeting. I myself, like many people of different faiths – and no faith – had been extremely disturbed (to say the least) by Israel's actions in Gaza already in the summer of 2006, when bridges and power stations were destroyed there in retaliation for the firing of rockets into Israeli territory. A year earlier, of course, Israel had withdrawn its forces from Gaza and dismantled settlements inhabited by thousands of Israelis. But the destruction of Gaza's bridges and power stations struck me and many Jews around the world as both immoral and idiotic, seemingly designed to plunge Gaza into greater poverty and distress.

That was there. Here in South London the reality is that my

congregation was founded by local South London Jews in 1929, two decades before the state of Israel even came into existence. Some of my members have been to Israel, a few are Israelis, and quite a few have relatives in Israel. But I could make those same statements in relation to France, Australia, Canada, Scotland, and the USA. Many of my members have never been to Israel at all. Just like other people, we tend to focus on the challenges facing us in our everyday lives right here in London. Some may think, 'I'm with Israel, right or wrong' – I have never heard anyone actually say that – but far more take a different view. My community has raised money for Palestinian healthcare and educational projects, ceaselessly done its bit to promote peace initiatives in the Middle East, and vigorously pursued meaningful inter faith relationships for nearly eight decades.

When, on 7 July 2005, bombs went off on trains and buses across London, I had also been on my way to my synagogue to open up for an inter faith event: our annual *faithsounds* concert. The bombs halted me in my tracks and forced the cancellation of the evening. They also put an end to the life of Miriam Hyman, a young woman from a family with deep roots in our congregation, killed on the bus at Tavistock Square. But the strength of local inter faith commitment meant that the *faithsounds* concert went ahead at a later date in 2005. And in July 2006, a year to the day after the 7/7 bombs, my synagogue was the site of *faithsounds III*, dedicated to the memory of Miriam Hyman.

And so the peace mala appeared at South London Liberal Synagogue, Streatham. A rope. A weighty, braided thing of fibre, entwined with coloured ribbons and messages. And people of other faiths, other South London communities, brought it to us – this intriguing object – into our 'house of meeting', our synagogue. We were shocked and bereft at that moment, yes. Thinking of those dead Palestinian children, their grieving families; thinking that some unknown person(s) saw us as child-killers; thinking of the anniversary marked that very day, 9 November, the *Kristallnacht* of 1938, when the Nazis burnt down hundreds of synagogues throughout Germany and Austria; and thinking of our own powerfully contrasting anniversary – for it was at the same time, November 1938, that my synagogue community moved into its building in Prentis Road, Streatham, our home to this day. And I myself was also thinking in particular of those in our community who had witnessed what happened on the Continent: our refugees, the men and women who managed to get out of Germany and central Europe in the late 1930s, most of them children and adolescents at the time. They found a new home here in South London, but in most cases their parents vanished into the death camps, never to be seen again. My greatest fear on that Thursday afternoon in November 2006 was that the refugees' group might be having its meeting that very day – and thus these old people, all of them very dear to me (my own grandparents were refugees from Nazi Germany), would be confronted by the sight of a defaced synagogue building. But their meeting was on another Thursday, a week later: after the posters had been taken away by the police; after Catriona and Sarah had appeared on our doorstep on the eve of Shabbat, the Sabbath, with the peace mala; and after the children in our *cheder* (the traditional synagogue school, on Sunday morning) had decorated the mala with their own messages of love and friendship; after a statement in support of our community had been signed by so many good people in other faith communities in South London; after numerous other messages of support and indignation had been received by us – most notably, from Toaha Qureshi of Stockwell, at that moment in far-away Pakistan; and after I had taken the peace mala myself to Southwark Cathedral for the prayers on the anniversary of 11 November 1918, the end of the four-year nightmare once thought of as the war to end all wars.

The Hebrew word *nechamah*, like so many Hebrew words, has a more or less straightforward translation in English – comfort, solace – and yet, like so many Hebrew words, it means so much more. It evokes the power of divine consolation which can touch our lives with healing and tenderness when we most need it – and it was symbolised for me by a strange, heavy rope, garlanded with ribbons and tags.

Further reading

Clapham and Stockwell Faith Forum: www.csff.co.uk.
Connect: Different Faiths, Shared Values, London: Inter Faith Network for the UK, www.interfaith.org.uk.
Forgiveness Project: www.theforgivenessproject.com.
Home Ground, 2005, special edition of community news magazine, August, www.stockwellpark.com/home-ground/home-ground-6a.pdf.
Joanne O'Brien and Martin Palmer, 2007, *The Atlas of Religion: Mapping contemporary challenges and beliefs*, London: Earthscan.
Deborah Orr, 2005, 'The Strength of My Shattered Community', *Indepen-*

dent, 26 July, http://comment.independent.co.uk/commentators/deborah_orr/article301626.ece.

Peace Mala, Wales: www.peacemala.org.uk.

St Ethelburga's Centre for Reconciliation & Peace: www.stethelburgas.org.

South London Inter Faith Group: www.southlondoninterfaith.org.uk.

Tchenka Jane Sunderland, 'Walking the Labyrinth', privately published, available from Norwich Cathedral bookshop.

Turkoman Gers (yurt hire), Parlour Cottage, Middle Hill Farm, Chalford Hill, Gloucestershire, GL6 8BE, 01452 771212.

Appendix 1

Statement after the police shooting on 22 July, 2005:

Stockwell Green Muslim Centre has played a central role in Stockwell Faith Forum from its inception in the summer of 2001.

Each year we hold a peace event at the local Stockwell Festival. This year, two days after 7th July, people of many faiths joined to form a human peace mala. A rope formed a strong circle. The colours attached to the rope represented our different faith traditions. All those present held the rope and declared:

'Our multi-faith community flourishes.
We celebrate our diversity.
No act of aggression will break us apart.'

Stockwell Faith Forum unreservedly condemns the recent bombings in London. We give our full support to the emergency services in serving and protecting all members of the community.

We stand in solidarity with members of Stockwell Green Muslim Centre to work for a cohesive, peaceful and just society.

Catriona Robertson, Chairperson, 22nd July 2005

Appendix 2

Statement in response to events at South London Liberal Synagogue, Friday 10 November 2006:

Clapham and Stockwell Faith Forum stands with the Rabbi and congregation of South London Liberal Synagogue in strongly denouncing the affixing of large photographs to the front of the Synagogue of Palestinian women and children killed by Israeli army action this week.

Many of us, from all faiths, are deeply concerned about events in the

Middle East. We deplore the action which led to the loss of innocent civilian life in Gaza on Wednesday night. But strength of feeling in no way justifies action of this kind outside a local synagogue.

Since its foundation in 1929, South London Liberal Synagogue, along with other Jewish organisations, has played a key role in promoting inter faith understanding – hosting concerts, lectures and many activities which are open to people of all faiths and of none.

The Faith Forum supports action which brings people together and does not drive them apart. Under no circumstances should we allow actions such as this to divide the community. Lambeth has a very diverse population. People from different religious and cultural traditions live side by side peaceably and work well together. The perpetrators of this action are out of step with public feeling. We want to export the peace, not import the wars.

Catriona Robertson, Toaha Qureshi, Jasmine Read, David Hart

Note

1 *The Koran*, 1974, translated by N. J. Dawood, fourth revised edition, Harmondsworth: Penguin, p. 275.

5 Healing Together

Sharing sacred space at the Queen Elizabeth Hospital

GEORGIANA HESKINS

with responses by Imrana Ghumra,
Qaisra Khan and Usman Ali

In everything do to others as you would have them do to you;
for this is the law and the prophets.

Matthew 7.12

None of you truly believes until he wishes for his brother what
he wishes for himself.

Number 13 of a collection of 43 sayings of Prophet Muhammad
(PBUH) known as Al-Nawawi's Forty Hadiths[1]

Six years ago, on my way to a blood test, I walked into the little
lobby area intended as a Prayer Room in our new-build NHS
hospital. It seemed an unpromising place and was seldom used.
Even the chaplain chose to pray elsewhere. The story of its
becoming 'sacred space' – a wellspring for spiritual healing in a
busy acute hospital – parallels the wider journey of chaplains
and volunteers learning to encounter God in one another and in
staff, patients and visitors from different faith traditions and
from none. In a national context where there is an increasing
interest in spirituality, and relatively few people who say they
are religious, chaplains try to support a wide variety of spiritual
quests. A chance encounter in the Prayer Room may well provide the starting point.

Patterns for prayer

The Prayer Room journey began with the chaplains' need to establish a home-base, not only for weekly gatherings, but for personal reflection and prayer – a daily rhythm for themselves and for other staff absorbing the distress and pain of others. Then came more team members, a prayer board, and a spider plant, and chaplains started to say their prayers in the room and waited for others to join them. Gradually regular users began to emerge and to establish their own patterns. Unlikely space became a place of prayerful encounter as it was used for its intended purpose and we began to learn that just calling it a 'Prayer Room' doesn't make it one.

At the beginning of each day someone lights a candle and individuals – including me – pause for a time of prayer and to read the scriptures. There is a shelf by the door with the holy books of most major faiths. We don't, in the mornings, try to say any communal prayer, but usually share the space with others also pausing on the way to their place of work, conscious that ward staff, on an early shift, have been there before us, and people with out-patients' appointments will soon be dropping in. By mid-morning there are often two or three people looking either for a moment's peace or for a listening ear from one of the chaplains. At 11 a.m., on mid-week mornings, the Hindu shrine is erected, the oil lamp is lit, and puja proceeds with chanting, the ringing of a bell and, occasionally, some incense. The Hindu chaplain is joined by a volunteer or the family of a patient – and together they proceed from the Prayer Room to the wards. At midday the Christians pause. This time we say prayers together and sing a hymn – following a traditional Christian 'office' – and we are sometimes joined by other colleagues and visitors. It's not a good time for patients – that's just when lunchtime is under way on the wards – but this middle part of the day provides welcome respite for staff. Muslim staff and visitors tend to make most use of the Prayer Room during the early afternoon. At the end of the working day we all pause again on the way home, to do salat or to write a prayer card – or to read those left by others. The room remains open throughout the night.

To this day the Prayer Room remains pretty bare of decoration. This is deliberate – so as not to impose distracting religious symbolism on one another. Some of us value natural objects and artefacts to help us to pray: shells, plants and pebbles can usually be found on the window sills. Both qiblah and cross are discreetly there, but we have chosen to keep all other religious symbolism to a minimum. The main exception to this is the bookcase where the scriptures sit. Other religious objects are, for their safety, kept elsewhere: Lord Buddha lives in the vestry (a small room used for storage and personal conversation next door) where his calming presence graces many an encounter. Very many of those whom the chaplains meet in hospital have a profound sense of being on a spiritual journey and yet struggle with the specifics of following a particular religious path. Proselytism is no part of a chaplain's task, so, although each of us is authorised by our own faith community, our services must be available to everyone. The hospitality of the Prayer Room is particularly appreciated by those for whom traditional religious symbolism has become barren.

Models of ministry

The Queen Elizabeth Hospital (the QE) on Woolwich Common opened in February 2001 on the site of an old military hospital. It replaced two acute hospitals serving a local South London community. Both had their own chapels but made no particular provision for religious practice other than Christian. A Muslim colleague, moving to the new hospital, did not know of the Prayer Room's existence and continued, like others, to make her own arrangements. Better signage, in languages other than English, made a big difference. Getting 'official' hospital signs took time – but our own home-made posters in Arabic, Urdu and Punjabi have served us well. There never has been a 'chapel' at the new QE, but it has been hard to shed the concept or the name. We are a PFI (Private Finance Initiative) hospital, and health service diversity requirements don't filter easily to our private sector partner companies. Just when we think the idea of a multi faith 'Prayer Room' has taken hold, suddenly cleaning rotas, notice boards and works schedules reassert the word 'Chapel' to remind us how deeply the concept is embedded in complex systems. Changing the culture is like turning a juggernaut.

When I arrived at the QE as a temporary locum chaplain, the chaplaincy team was entirely Christian. Two Catholic priests came in to visit and there were two whole-time posts, both held by Anglicans, of whom I was one. Like most Church of England priests I had learned pastoral ministry in a parish setting. When I started at the hospital I found that the list of local faith leaders, drawn up by a previous locum chaplain, had been used to call people in only when requested, and that there was little continuity or opportunity for dialogue with faith leaders other than Christian.

We needed a team of trained healthcare chaplains who understood NHS ways; yet our models of ministry were so very different. I remember one of our early training sessions, designed for volunteers to learn 'listening skills', being hijacked by a newcomer to the team, who had come to learn strategies for 'making people listen' – to him. As a Muslim teacher he was accustomed to interpreting the sacred texts, and the very notion of a 'pastoral' ministry – in the Christian sense – was novel. The religious and liturgical crossovers were never straightforward either. The Hindu chaplain had to explain to me that he was not a 'funeral priest' when I asked him to assist me with the burial of a baby. (Whereas adult Hindus are cremated, babies are buried, and if a specialist funeral priest is not available then the rituals are arranged by the family.) The imams do not manage the administration of the mosque and it's been complicated knowing the appropriate person to approach for different kinds of assistance. The teaching role is paramount in Islam, and for our Hindu priest ritual duties come first. The Sikh priest is entirely confined to the Gurdwara, and other Sikh volunteers are able to provide all the religious care needed in hospital. These different models of ministry are not, of course, cast in stone, and there is a great deal of overlap between the duties of different kinds of faith leader, but the differences between the ways in which we have been trained are phenomenally wide and we've all been on a rich learning curve.

While our new team was beginning to form so Muslim prayer on Friday was gathering a regular congregation. One of the doctors led the prayer and prepared a short *khutba* (sermon) each week. Numbers grew and the Jum'a (Friday Prayer) group suggested that the Mosque might provide an imam to do the teaching. The relationship with the Greenwich Islamic Centre developed, and a series of teachers, registered as hospital volunteers, have acted as Muslim advisors within the chaplaincy team. We were keen to recruit some female volunteers, so, accompanied by a QE colleague, I went to the women's Arabic class at the Mosque. Our volunteer team has since grown to include

Muslims, both women and men, with an impressive range of mother-tongue languages between them. Recently, at Friday prayer, staff and patients were glad to welcome two NHS managers: the Director of Nursing and the Director of Clinical Services, whose words and presence provided reassurance to medical staff at a time when 'extremism' was much in the news. It was a tiny sign of the way in which chaplains, working together, can broker pastoral and religious care in a secular context.

Communication and inter faith insight

Sikh, Hindu and Muslim volunteers now visit regularly along-side the Christians; sometimes they take responsibility for a particular area of the hospital, and sometimes they use their language skills to untangle difficult situations. One such occurred when a Christian nurse, with experience back home in Nigeria of violent conflict between Christians and Muslims, was preparing a Sikh patient for theatre. She was terrified by his kirpan (small ritual sword), unaware of its religious significance, and reliving the trauma of her childhood. A Sikh volunteer defused the immediate situation and was able to offer support and training to the ward staff and their manager – as well as reassurance, in Punjabi, for the patient. Other awkward situations have included the Catholic patient who was 'teased' by a nurse for keeping a small Buddha beside his bed on the eve of a significant operation. To be told that 'Jesus is the only Way' was clearly unprofessional and inappropriate. Chaplaincy was able to feed back our concern to the member of staff concerned. Once, an authorised Hindu volunteer was denied access to a patient on what seemed spurious grounds. Thanks to her willingness to withdraw courte-ously, and bring the incident to a discussion in the team, it was resolved.

More often the cross-cultural dialogue feels entirely positive. We remember the conversations with a terminally ill Sikh woman who herself began to talk about the suffering and pain of Jesus. The same patient – and others – have reacted with great joy to a laminated picture of Guru Nanak taken off the internet and pasted to a wall by their bed. In the Critical Care Unit a patient's wife taped the picture so that he could see it without turning and thanked us for our prayers, saying: 'After all, there is only one God.' In the Prayer Room we feel the benefit of Muslim doctors

and other staff praying in the regular way they do, sensing that
simple reorientation of their whole self symbolised in physical
prostration; then the quiet sitting – redirection towards God
alone. We remember the Sri Lankan Buddhist patient, who was
dying, and who valued Christian prayers. When she was here
one of the chaplains would carry the Buddha statue through the
hospital like a baby, getting many an interested look, so that she
could have the statue on the shelf in her room. All of us continue
to marvel, when we come into the Prayer Room, at the two or
three people from totally different religious backgrounds praying in their own ways – and yet together.

Working together and praying together

In the Accident and Emergency department our work is essentially pastoral rather than religious. We work in pairs that tran-
scend religious and cultural difference: a Pentecostal Ghanaian
Christian and a Somali Muslim, a Hindu with a Sikh. There are
weekly opportunities to de-brief and a monthly reflection and
training session has given us all the chance to learn from one
another. Gradually we have undertaken the pastoral training
essential to hospital chaplaincy, and this has been enriched by
insights very different from the western medical model (originally Christian), with its individualism and focus on 'mending'
what is 'broken', rather as if the body were a machine made up of
disparate parts. Finding meaning in illness, a more corporate and
relational model – a sense that life extends into other lives, that
grief may be public, and that medicine may be holistic – these are
the fruits of our ongoing discussions with one another. Because
many of us work together anyway we have good reason to cross
paths on a daily basis. Staff members who use the Prayer Room
have a shared interest in healthcare – in the fullest, spiritual sense
– and a real chance, therefore, to share insights and problems as
they come up. Communication (as one of the Muslim volunteers
comments in his reflection below) really is the key. I truly hope
that we shall increasingly understand and respect each other's
beliefs and practices.

The pattern of corporate worship in the Prayer Room serves
Christians, Hindus and Muslims, and observers sometimes
become participants: one day Rafiq, a Hindu doctor, chose to
remain during our simple Eucharist – an attentive, gracious pres-

ence. Members of the chaplaincy team sometimes sit in with one another: learning to value the orderliness of Jum'a, the rich sensuality of Puja, the mystery of Eucharist, or the simplicity of a midday office. Having said that, we try to keep 'gatherings' to a minimum. One of the joys of the Prayer Room journey, so far, has been the enriching experience of shared silence as we learn greater sensitivity to each other's needs. On a small trellis which screens the main doorway the notices ask us to 'Pause for a moment', 'Come in quietly' and 'Give others space'. Recently, Christians gathering for the Eucharist were witnesses to salat as Muslims slipped in to pray at their appointed time, and we all, as we greeted each other, were given a new sense of the One-ness of Allah.

Hospitality and solitude

The Prayer Room is accessibly situated on the main corridor – en route both for the wards and for the Out Patients department. This creates a passing trade from visitors, from staff, and from patients in the nearby mental health unit. Our Prayer Room, by contrast with most other local places of worship, is always open, and we occasionally get visitors, otherwise unrelated to the hospital, popping in with flowers on an anniversary – or, as recently, a Buddhist needing somewhere to pray after the sudden death of her brother-in-law in Sri Lanka. This provoked the interesting, but not unusual, encounter between several traditions when the Buddha image, donated by the local Chinese temple, came into his own as the focus for her devotions, and she used the sandy Lenten 'desert' of the Christians in which to plant her candle. Alerted by the chaplaincy, it was a Chinese Buddhist who took her to the Temple, initiating a new pastoral collaboration.

Much of the activity normally associated with places of worship is to do with gathering a faith community together. As we follow the seasons of the year in hospital I'm very aware that what we offer has to be available to individuals slipping alone into the Prayer Room at odd times before work, in tea-breaks, between shifts, or at visiting time. We have found that Divali, World Aids Day, Ramadan, Eid, Ash Wednesday, Palm Sunday, and the season of Remembrance, can all be adapted for this drop-in trade. Nutritious dates for Ifthaari (fast-breaking), a bowl of ashes and a paper towel, palm crosses and Holy Week devotions, red ribbons, bowls of water, fragrant oil, and cairns, may all be adapted for the visitor worshipping alone. Perhaps the most powerful resource is the prayer board, which seems to be popular with people of all faith traditions: small coloured cards, in a variety of languages, appear every day – a poignant reminder that a hospital is a place where life has been interrupted by accident or illness, birth or death. The Prayer Room gives everyone a chance to reflect.

Pressure on space

Not everyone values silence. The discreet murmurings of 'prayer partners' are more easily accommodated than intense conversation and some kinds of music. We are fortunate that our vestry and office space is easily accessible from the Prayer Room. Though we continue to marvel at the sacredness of shared space, it's nevertheless good to be able to offer an alternative during Mass, Jum'a, memorial services, or when family gatherings have needed the main room. A good example of this was the day I walked into the Prayer Room to find it gradually filling with grieving people – some of whom were coming in and going out again – accumulating, rather alarmingly, in our small space.

One of my fellow chaplains takes up the story:

I was called into A&E [the Accident and Emergency department] at about 8 a.m. on a weekday morning, after a fatal stabbing. The family was obviously distraught. There was a large group already present, including three adult children of the deceased. There were also several police officers in attendance. The family was Buddhist and felt the need to pray. I escorted them to the Prayer Room where it was explained to me that, in their tradition, they needed to have a service immediately. More and more members of the extended family were arriving in A&E so I advised the staff to send them all round to the Prayer Room. We were also able to offer space for the police to talk, privately, with family members. I offered one of our Buddhist contacts, but the family were in touch with their own priest. I also offered the use of our Buddha statue, but someone was bringing one from home. I made a pot of tea, brought water and put out cups and glasses. Members of the family were sent out to buy flowers, fruit and incense. By this time there were about seventy people in the Prayer Room (it ordinarily seats twenty). The family built a shrine and began their ceremony when the priest arrived.

At around the time that the Buddhist service began a number of our regular users appeared: Muslim women coming for their midday prayers. They used the vestry room, and as they were leaving two of them commented on how wonderful it was that there had been sufficient space both for themselves and for the grieving family. It was great that they were gracious, in using the alternative prayer room, so that the Buddhist rituals could take place.

Involving the community

The development of the Prayer Room has been supported by local faith communities. The Mosque, Sikh Gurdwara, Hindu Mandir and Buddhist Temple have contributed books, prayer mats, artefacts and furnishings – including a purpose-built shoe rack – and a wealth of useful advice. Our volunteers keep us connected with a variety of churches and congregations and we maintain an enthusiastic involvement with the Greenwich Multi-Faith Forum. These partnerships are very precious, and our chaplaincy volunteer team is beginning to reflect the personal links which extend to patients and their families. I hope that the Prayer Room will increasingly support this network for pastoral and spiritual care. It is not a chapel, still less a church, and nor is it a mosque or a temple; yet through it we endeavour to be hospitable to one another and to work together for the wholeness and healing of the hospital and wider community.

As part of the National Health Service we are committed to diversity and religious beliefs policies and of course we serve two London boroughs (Greenwich and Bexley) that are culturally very rich. As a result we have an amazing opportunity here at the QE for the Chaplaincy and Prayer Room to play a proactive role in mutual understanding. In conjunction with the hospital Arts Manager, we hold occasional events to coincide with religious festivals, and these are open to the public. An Eid gathering was well received, and we've held a Sikh festival, had Baha'i readings, and celebrated Divali. All have involved food, prayer and some explanation of traditional customs. For the New Year celebrations the Baha'is generously volunteered their labour to clear our garden courtyard and put up banners for the children's ward. Such collaborations have built new friendships in the community and, we hope, taken some of the dread and unfamiliarity out of coming into hospital.

Finally

Sometimes chaplains and volunteers are able to offer religious and sacramental care to people of our own faith community, and sometimes we can extend this to people who share our cultural background or language; but there are many occasions when we find ourselves in totally unfamiliar territory, and this takes a particular kind of skill and sensitivity. Each of us is such a complex mixture of background and ethnicity, language and culture, that we can never hope to know for sure what will contribute to someone else's healing. This is where the chaplain's dictum, 'listening is the highest form of hospitality,'[2] really comes into its own: listening to one another, learning from patients and their families, and allowing ourselves to be led by our intuition. These very ordinary requirements of any chaplain are even more crucial in a multi faith context. Six years on – and nothing happens overnight – we are discovering that there is potential in the chance encounters and happy accidents of sharing sacred space.

Responses

By Imrana Ghumra, manager of the Healthcare Library QEH:

Using the prayer room has been an educational experience for me. While waiting, either for the ablution facility to become free or for prayer groups to finish, you can see how the room is used so diversely. Sometimes I have been approached by people who have observed my prayers and commented on a similar concept within their faith or how their faith recognises the teachings of our Prophet Muhammad (peace be upon him).

By Qaisra Khan, Chaplaincy Co-ordinator for Oxleas Mental Health Trust:

I have visited the prayer room at the QE on a number of occasions: generally for work but sometimes to find a welcoming
place where I can be and meet the team who, no matter how
busy, are always happy to have a cup of tea. It's a place that is
rarely empty and where I have been able to enter and join
Muslims and Christians in prayer.

I am very aware that my enthusiasm for multi faith working
has been a developing journey, and sometimes it is good to be
reminded of the things that stop me in my tracks and make me
reflect. I had quite a surprise in the QE Prayer Room when, during Christmas, there was a huge nativity structure. As a Muslim
I have come to associate the nativity scene with school and
Christmas shopping. I was also a bit thrown by visiting during
Friday Prayers for the first time. The sheer number of people
made it different from my previous experience. Of course it's
good that so many use the room, but it could have been a bit
intimidating if you weren't expecting it.

The prayer room at the QE is a great resource right at the heart
of the hospital, rather than being tucked away in a corner. The
activity and its welcoming nature also provide an invaluable
resource to Oxleas House (the neighbouring mental health unit)
where I work.

By Usman Ali, volunteer at QEH:

We tend to change the prayer room (for Friday Prayer) to make
maximum use of the space. Sometimes others, who are not
Muslims, come in to pray and listen. I have been approached by
non-Muslims to lend my ear, and sometimes they say 'Pray for
me,' knowing that I am from a different faith. The long beard
links me to Islam. They see me as a man of religion and are
comfortable enough to speak to me.

I have visited many prayer rooms in various hospitals in
London and, without being biased, the prayer room at the QE is
unique in that it is not known as a 'multi faith prayer room' or
'chapel' but just as a 'prayer room'. I believe this makes it different because it's used by people of so many faiths during the week
– and one might not realise it. What also makes it comfortable is

the fact that there are no obvious religious symbols; and, if on occasion there are, we often move or cover them – but with each other's consent.

The prayer room is also a quiet area, where people can get away from the hustle and bustle of the hospital. Often I have seen doctors taking a nap, staff relaxing, and patients just taking a moment or two.

The chaplaincy team work together, hand in hand, because we have the most important tool, and that is communication. We are able to talk to each other face to face, email, phone and so on, and we are open with each other even on the most sensitive issues. This leads us to debate, discuss and understand each other's point of view (not only on religious matters), and we are able to support each other.

Further reading

Mark Cobb, 2005, *The Hospital Chaplain's Handbook*, Norwich: Canterbury Press.

Susan Hollins, 2006, *Religions, Culture and Healthcare: A Practical Handbook for Use in Healthcare Environments*, Abingdon: Radcliffe Publishing.

Helen Orchard (ed.), 2001, *Spirituality in Health Care Contexts*, London: Jessica Kingsley.

Notes

1 www.isna.net/services/library/hadith/hadithnabawi.html#hadith13.

2 Henri Nouwen, 1976, *Reaching Out: The three movements of the spiritual life*, Glasgow: William Collins, pp. 68–9.

6 Facing death together

A multi faith funeral

ALISON PRICE

with a response by Iffat Rizvi

[God] will wipe every tear from their eyes.
Death will be no more;
mourning and crying and pain will be no more . . .

Revelation 21.4

Recognise that there is only one race and that is of human beings.

Guru Gobind Singh, 1666–1708, the last of the ten Sikh Gurus[1]

On an overcast Friday morning in May 2003, as usual for a church funeral, I led the coffin through the west doors and down the long aisle to the chancel steps. On this long journey I had time to reflect on why my heart was beating faster than normal. It was because this funeral was not going to be a 'run of the mill' service, and as I reached the chancel steps and turned to face the congregation the visual impact highlighted its uniqueness. First, there were many young people in the congregation, reflecting the age of the deceased and the tragic circumstances in which she had lost her life; and second, there was a sea of pale-coloured saris.

In one way I shouldn't have been surprised at the make-up of the congregation because it reflected the various faith communities who live in the parish in which I serve as Vicar. The surprise was that they were in my church and I was officiating at a funeral of a murdered woman whose mother is a Sikh and father a Muslim.

The young woman had been murdered back in March. Shockwaves had quickly run through the local community as the news of the death of this twenty-five-year-old trickled out.

Her family live opposite my church and I was on nodding acquaintance with them. Once I heard the news I went over to visit them. It was heart-breaking to see the mother struggling to accept that her only daughter was dead and comprehend the 'how?' and the 'why?' of the tragedy.

I was a little surprised but rather pleased to be asked by the family to take the funeral: to be the officiant at this service was going to be challenging on many levels. My overriding objective was to support these members of my parish who had come to me for help in their terrible time of need. At the same time, I needed to maintain my own integrity as an Anglican priest.

The mother and I had a number of meetings and gradually the funeral service started to take shape. One of the early problems was that we didn't know when the funeral would take place, because the body wasn't being released by the coroner before all the forensic and autopsy requirements had been carried out. This wait was hard enough in itself, but in Muslim tradition the body of a deceased person should be interfered with as little as possi-ble and the funeral should be within twenty-four hours of the death. This funeral took place sixty-two days after the death.

My meetings with the mother were in her front room where a large picture of her daughter was on display surrounded by flowers. The photograph reflected the mother's description of her daughter: beautiful and happy with her life before her. It seemed that the daughter didn't practise any particular religion but she was a spiritual person and was moved by living in the shadow of my church. Many of her friends wanted to make contributions to the service as a way of paying their respects to the friend they had so unexpectedly lost in the small hours of a March morning: so this humanitarian dimension, along with the Sikh and Muslim traditions and my own Christian integrity, had to be included in the service. Bearing all this in mind, the funeral service sheet was entitled 'A Funeral and Humanitarian Service'.

I needed to go back to basics and remind myself what a funeral service is aiming to do. First, it is to commend the deceased to God; second, to bring comfort to the family; and third, for the body to be disposed of with respect and dignity. Starting with the final point: for Muslims a body must be buried with the deceased facing the holy city of Makkah, and for Sikhs the ideal is cremation with the ashes submerged in a river. The final decision was that the deceased was to be placed in an above-ground vault.

In the Christian tradition we commend the soul of the deceased to God through Jesus Christ who through his resurrection opened the gate of heaven to all who believe, so that the deceased can enjoy eternal life with God. Muslims too believe in eternal life and that the soul leaves the body at the moment of death; and prayers include asking for God's mercy to be with the departed. The words from the Qur'an used at the graveside have the same flavour as the Christian words of committal.

Sikhs see death as a natural process and according to God's will, and prayers over the body are said in this vein. The soul does not die; rather, death is a progression of the soul on its journey to God through a series of rebirths.

For many today, bringing comfort to the bereaved is not channelled through the traditions of a particular faith but rather through secular music that held significance for the deceased and through tributes about his or her life. With all funerals I believe there needs to be a balance; purely focusing on secular songs and being told how nice and kind a person was provides little of substance for those grieving to focus on and a rather superficial understanding of hope and comfort.

Now that I had it very clearly in my mind what the funeral was to achieve, I felt in a better place to help the mother compile all her thoughts and ideas into some sort of order that she was happy with and that would meet my objectives. The running order for the service went as follows. After the welcome, the Henry Scott Holland poem 'All Is Well' was to be read. Many families choose to have this particular poem read at a funeral service, and I know I am not the only cleric to have some problems with it, mainly because of the first line, 'Death is nothing at all'. Death in any circumstances is not 'nothing at all', and certainly not in this case when we were dealing with a twenty-five-year-old who was shot dead. But the poem does have redeeming phrases in it where it talks about remembering the person as they were, calling them by their 'old familiar name', and about the fact that just because a person is out of sight it doesn't mean that they are out of mind. The service then would continue with a number of testimonies from family and friends, interspersed with music, mostly from CDs. Just to get all this music played in the right order was going to be no mean feat, but I knew I could rely on one of my teenage servers not to get flustered or make a mess of it. Once we knew the date of the funeral I had to write to his college to ask for him to have the day off, and thankfully they agreed.

The specifically Christian material that was used included a reading from 1 Corinthians 13, reminding us what love means and that at the moment we only see God dimly, but that in time, when we die, we will have the chance to see God face to face. The congregation were to say the traditional words of the Lord's Prayer and I was to use the Christian words for the commendation.

Both the mother and I felt the service would give people the opportunity to pay their respects and also to grieve the death of this young woman. On the front cover of the order of service were the symbols of the major world faiths.

It had taken some time to compile the service, and still we didn't know when the body was going to be released. By now Easter was fast approaching, and on Easter Saturday I was due to get married and go on two weeks' honeymoon. So before I left I had to brief my colleague in the neighbouring parish, in case the body was released. It would then have been possible for the funeral to go ahead while I was away, disappointing though it would have been for me not to take the service, having got to know the family so well.

Well, at least I got to know the deceased's mother extremely well, and her two brothers – but her father was never involved in our discussions. I suspect he was dealing with what would happen at the mosque, and coping with his own grief in his own way and through his own beliefs and tradition. For the mother it seemed that the planning and putting together of the funeral service gave her a focus and a specific way to express her love for her daughter and the grief she felt.

Because of the Sikh belief that death is a natural process and part of God's will and thus that the deceased are progressing on their journey to God, public displays of grief are discouraged. Personal grieving at home is channelled through prayers, ideally with others, as this brings comfort. This might be manageable when the loved one who has died had lived a full and active life and died peacefully at a good age. But when you are not only grieving the loss of your beautiful young daughter on the threshold of life, but also trying to piece together how it was that she came to be shot at point-blank range through a car window, then not giving way to your grief, publicly or privately, is practically an impossible task.

In the Muslim tradition, also, too much outward showing of grief is discouraged, as Allah is the One who gives life and takes it away and it is therefore not for believers to question that. Traditionally, western Christians also 'put on a brave face' and are commended if they do not weep publicly. An emphasis on thanksgiving for the life of the deceased is encouraged, as is the conviction that they will now be at rest in God's presence, which is cause for rejoicing. Christians from other cultures such as African and Caribbean are much more likely to express their emotions openly and publicly.

Many cultures and faith traditions have specified times of mourning. This seems a good idea so that those who are bereaved and those who want to support them each know what to do and what to expect. In Muslim tradition official mourning lasts three days. There is an increase in devotion, and the bereaved receive visitors who bring their offers of condolences. On the third day the relatives visit the grave and recite extracts from the Qur'an. In Sikh tradition the initial mourning period lasts for ten to fourteen days, and during this time the entire Sri Guru Granth Sahib, the Sikh holy writings, are read. 'Official' mourning may then last another couple of weeks, during which the women and men continue to wear sober-coloured clothes and turbans. In present-day western Christian practice there is no such formal custom or guidance. The Letter of James in the Bible bids us 'to care for widows and orphans in their distress',[2] but it is up to the individual to decide how to do that and those on the sidelines often don't know what to say or don't want to intrude and so pass by on the other side, leaving the bereaved feeling even more isolated and lonely.

Because of the length of time between the death and the funeral of this woman none of the traditional customs fitted the circumstances and, without these comforting structures of bereavement, the loss and confusion of the family were intensified.

At last the day came when the body was released and the date could be set for the funeral – in the second week after my return from honeymoon. Thankfully the mother and I had done all the hard work towards the service, so now it was just a matter of finalising and fine-tuning the arrangements. There was to be other religious input in the final goodbye to the family's beloved daughter, and in these I would not play a significant part because they were to do with the parents' beliefs and customs.

To prepare a body for burial it is the custom for both Muslims

and Sikhs that the family should wash and dress the deceased
ready for the funeral, and that prayers should be said over the
body at home. These prayers can be led either by their respective
religious leaders or by a family member. In Sikh tradition, on the
way to the funeral hymns are sung that encourage a feeling of
detachment to aid the family in not showing grief.

As the morning of the funeral dawned I felt I had quite a day
ahead of me. How much more so for the parents who were to
bury their only daughter. The arrangement was that I would go
to the house just before the funeral to accompany the body over
to church. But first there were the more mundane tasks to be
done, such as getting the church ready, briefing my competent
teenager server with his duties, and having a word with those
setting up the hall for the refreshments.

Once I felt I was as ready as I could be for such a service, I went
over to the family home. Lots of people had already gathered,
and I managed to work my way through the front door of the
house, past numerous staff from the undertakers, and into the
room where the open coffin was, surrounded by members of
the family. The noise was a cacophony of prayers, crying, and
general chatter. It would soon be time for the service to begin,
and the funeral director was trying desperately to encourage the
family to allow him to replace the lid of the coffin and make the
journey over to church for the next stage in this epic farewell. I
nipped ahead of the family to finish robing and then I met them
at the west doors of the church, just a stone's throw from their
front door. Once I was at the chancel steps and the coffin was
in its place I realised that the father was not present. I wasn't
entirely sure whether his intention was to come into the church
or just to attend the ceremony which was to follow at the
mosque. I quickly weighed up what was best to do, and decided
to have a word with the mother. There then followed a brief
hiatus as the father was fetched. Now we could get under way
the service went along smoothly; all the various bits of music
were played in the right place, and the tributes by family and
friends were well done and moving.

As I led the coffin back down the long aisle to the west door I
could relax a little as the main part of the day for which I was
responsible had gone smoothly. The people gathered had been
given a chance to say goodbye to their friend and family member
within a framework of hope of eternal life. I saw the coffin away
from the church on to the next part of the day's proceedings:

Friday prayers at the local mosque. Those people not going to the mosque were offered lunch in the church hall. I went back to the vicarage for a quiet lunch to recover and get myself ready for the final act of farewell to this beloved daughter.

Soon it was time to hop on my bike and pedal to the cemetery. When the family arrived the crowd of people had grown significantly, with those from the mosque joining us. The vault where the body was to be laid was right at the far side of the cemetery. I found myself standing next to the imam at its entrance. I appreciated that it must have been very hard for him to share the final act of committal with an Anglican cleric, and with a woman. There was a brief discussion before I said my words of committal, then the imam said his, and then twenty-five white doves were released. These final few minutes of the day's proceedings encapsulated the aspects which had to be incorporated so that all might feel that they had had their chance to say their farewell to their friend, niece, cousin, sister, and daughter.

As we all stood gazing heavenward, watching the twenty-five doves fly away, I pondered what happened to the doves. Did they go now and live a life of freedom, and would they survive it? Afterwards the dove-keeper informed me that they would be home before him, waiting for their tea. I wondered if there was something in that flight home to the familiar that could be reflected in death: a return to the one who had created us and in whose image we are made. The metaphor feels welcoming and even exciting.

There was no more time to stand there gazing into heaven. Everyone was now going back to the church hall where refreshments were being served and there was a more informal time for family and friends to chat over their memories of this beautiful young woman. Yet still the unanswered question 'Why?' hung in the air.

It is through my church hall that most of our contacts with local people of other faiths take place. They use the large space for weddings, naming ceremonies, funerals, coming of age festivities, and general gatherings. But it was this funeral that gave me the most intense involvement with people of other faiths. Everyone could identify and empathise with the heartbreak of this family losing their daughter in tragic circumstances. And it seems it is that which unites people. How different faith traditions deal with such a situation seems of secondary importance.

The suffering of fellow human beings in our midst is the unifying point, and particularly in this case we as a church were happy for our premises to be used by people of other faith traditions.

When I was chaplain to the Mayor of Merton a couple of years later we hosted an inter faith service that was well attended by members of my congregation. It is such situations that make us all realise that within our own culture and tradition we are all trying to do our best to bring up our families, earn a living, and worship our God, to the best of our abilities. It is when unity is seen in action that I believe we get a glimpse of God's Kingdom. However, having a watered-down religion in order to try to keep everyone happy, with the hope of not offending anyone, is not right. The way forward, in my view, is that as Christians we need to be clear what it is that makes up our integrity and what it is to which we must hold firmly. That is how we will gain the respect of people who practise another faith, for usually they are very clear about what they believe and why.

As I write this chapter my time of ministry in this multi faith area comes to an end; I am having some time out to care for my new baby son and we shall be leaving London to live in Southampton, which also has a lively multi faith presence. I shall always be grateful for the experience and understanding of other faiths and cultures that the last eight years have offered me, and especially for the involvement with this particular family as they struggled to understand and grieve their daughter's untimely death. May she rest in peace.

Response by Iffat Rizvi

Reading the Revd Alison's chapter on the funeral of my daughter took me back to the day on which I was told that she was dead. My life just ended and I wanted the ground to open up and swallow me. How I was able to contain myself at the time I just don't know. The pain has never left me, but I have had to learn to deal with it and live for those who still need me, my two sons. Eighteen months after my daughter's death, my husband died from the pain and trauma of losing her.

I had never been involved in arranging anyone's funeral before. At the time both of my parents were still alive. The thought of having to arrange my daughter's funeral was unbearable and I wanted her back at home with me where she belonged.

What I did manage to focus on was the fact that I knew that the funeral had to reflect the person that my daughter was. I spent my early childhood in East Africa and my parents were Sikh. We came to England when I was eight years old; it was soon Christmas, and I found myself performing in the school nativity play. My father was so proud of me. It was through this background of acceptance and respect for all religions that my own thoughts and beliefs developed, with the emphasis being on the One God. This is how I brought up my own children. My daughter particularly took this on board and would often gather about her people of many different faiths. So I didn't want her funeral to be a Sikh funeral or a Muslim funeral. That didn't feel right. To reflect my daughter's life and beliefs the funeral needed to embrace as many religions as possible. The funeral needed to demonstrate that there is One God.

The reason I approached the Revd Alison to ask whether we could hold the service in St Barnabas' Church is that ever since we had moved to our house next door my daughter had always talked about the church being a special place for her: though I had always imagined that the specialness of the church was because she would get married there, not buried.

Having to prepare for the funeral service was a good focus in those early weeks, and despite the terrible pain I felt very connected with God and with my daughter. When I told my family and my husband's family, who are Muslims, that the funeral service was to be held at St Barnabas', there was some anxiety and questioning as to why it was to be held in a Christian place of worship; but I held on to my initial instinct, that I wanted this funeral to be my daughter's and to reflect her. I didn't want it to feel as if it could be anybody's funeral.

On the day of the funeral, the Sikh leader came to the house at seven o'clock to say prayers. I had already prepared my daughter's body for the funeral, bathing her and dressing her myself.

The church was full of people who mattered to my daughter and a huge spread of religions and cultures were represented. All those who came, and especially those who had expressed concern, including my husband, felt that the service was right. It was led with dignity and respect. It reflected the life and beliefs of my daughter. There was an overwhelming feeling of love and peace, and many said that this is how it should be: all the faiths worshipping together.

When the cortege went on to the Mosque, four funeral prayers instead of the usual one were recited, and the Imam spoke movingly about young death. Probably the most beautiful part of the services was seeing the Imam with the Revd Alison standing side by side as they said the final prayers for my beloved daughter. The Imam said that this funeral service had opened his eyes to how things could and might be: Muslims saying prayer in church and mosques being open to all people: and this in fact is what he did, opening his mosque to all people.

My daughter's funeral challenged people of all faiths in a loving way. And my daughter Sabina was all about love.

Further reading

W. Owen Cole (ed.), 1982/1991, *Five World Faiths*, London: Cassell.
Kenneth Cracknell, 2005, *In Good and Generous Faith: Christian Response to Religious Pluralism*, Norwich: Epworth Press.

The charity started by Sabina's mother is Sabina Trust Against Revolvers and Racism (STARR): www.starr-homicide.org.uk.

Notes

1 Guru Gobind Singh, *Akal Ustat*, 85, 1.4. See *Textual Studies for the Study of Sikhism*, 1984, trans. W. H. McLeod, Chicago: University of Chicago Press, section 3.2.2, for the *Akal Ustat*.

2 James 1.27.

7 In Training Together

A Hindu teaches Christians

ALAN GADD

with a response by Ganesh Lall

Then Peter began to speak to them: 'I truly understand that God shows no partiality, but in every nation anyone who fears him and does what is right is acceptable to him.'

Acts 10.34–5

I do not want my house to be walled in on all sides and my windows to be stuffed. I want the cultures of all lands to be blown about my house as freely as possible. But I refuse to be blown off my feet by any.

Mahatma Gandhi[1]

I have some significant memories from the first time I sat in on a session where Ganesh Lall was teaching Christians. I wasn't myself surprised, though I think most of the group were, when at an early stage in the session Ganesh affirmed the oneness of God in Hindu understanding. Most Christians assume that the diversity of forms in which God is acknowledged by Hindus negates the oneness of God, but this is not the case. I *was* surprised, however, when he went on to call into question the very term 'Hinduism'. He said that the term represents a western construct that arose from experience of what should more accurately be called simply 'the religious tradition of India'. So there is really no 'faith' called 'Hinduism'. I realised then how fruitful it can be to learn about another religious tradition from someone who belongs to that tradition.

How it came about

That a Hindu was teaching Christians had come about through the Diocesan Inter Faith Group, set up in 1998 with a statement of purpose that I feel has stood the test of time very well:

> To enhance Christian understanding of other religious tradi-
> tions and promote good relationships between the Anglican
> Church in the Diocese of Southwark and peoples of other
> religious traditions in this geographical area, recognising the
> enrichment as well as the challenges which a multi-religious
> culture provides.

Part of the strategy for fulfilling this purpose was the provision of adequate training and educational opportunities; the group was therefore very pleased at the opportunity presented by a new Certificate in Christian Discipleship which was started by the Anglican Diocese of Southwark around the year 2000, along-side its existing Certificate in Biblical and Theological Studies. The new course was to employ a more experiential style of learn-ing, and was set up as a series of short modules, each consisting typically of five sessions. Canon Bruce Saunders, the Diocesan Missioner and at the time Chair of the Diocesan Inter Faith Group, worked with other members of the group to devise a module on Inter Faith Relationships. This was included in the course for the first time in September 2001 in Wimbledon.

Particularly important was the fourth session of the inter faith module, which was billed as 'a face to face encounter with some-one of another faith'. These were to prove very creative sessions for Christians with little previous inter faith experience. Sarah Thorley was often the member of the Diocesan Inter Faith Group who took responsibility for the fourth session, and it was Sarah who brought Ganesh Lall into this work.

Ganesh had come to Britain from Guyana in the 1950s. He was one of the 'founding fathers' of the Caribbean Hindu Cultural Society (CHCS) whose Temple is located in the Brixton Hill area of South London. He has a great commitment to improved understanding among people of different faith traditions, and has been a member for many years of the committee of the South London Inter Faith Group. From this involvement Ganesh was well qualified for the 'session four' role.

I myself have had the privilege of being present at this session on two occasions – in Eltham, and then near the Elephant and Castle – when Ganesh was filling the role of 'someone of another faith' so that there could be a 'face to face encounter'. I experienced an impressive quality in the way he approached the task. Some of that, of course, derives from his personal qualities, but we need also to note important features of his community heritage.

The Caribbean Hindu community

The South Asian population of the Caribbean has its origins in the indentured labour schemes of the British Empire in the nineteenth century. The indentured system was devised to fill the labour gap that resulted from the abolition of slavery. It was not so very different from slavery in the way people were treated. In fact, there is some justifiable feeling among the Caribbean Asian community in London that *their* history was overlooked in 2007 during the commemoration of the 200th anniversary of the Act of Parliament for the abolition of the slave trade.

Guyana and Trinidad & Tobago are the two Caribbean countries where the largest communities of South Asian people were established, though smaller groups are to be found in other islands. There is also a link with Mauritius, where the British piloted the indentured labour scheme before implementing it for the Caribbean plantations.

Among those who came to the Caribbean in this way, it is estimated that 90 per cent were Hindus and 10 per cent Muslims. The hardship and oppression they experienced gave them all a deep sense of their common humanity, and this must have contributed in a major way to the remarkable ease that people of different faiths have with one another. In the Caribbean context there was a further encounter, with various strands of Christianity, and the relaxed grassroots relationship among the faiths continued. It is not uncommon to find that a given family includes adherents of Hinduism, Islam and Christianity among its members.

These special multi faith contexts of Guyana and Trinidad & Tobago are plainly evident at the Caribbean Hindu Temple in Brixton Hill today. Ivor Smith-Cameron, a member of the Diocesan Inter Faith Group, told me about the experience of his first visit to the Wednesday lunch club at the Temple. He found himself chatting to a couple who numbered an archdeacon in Canada among their relations, and shortly afterwards met an Ismaili Muslim woman who, though not herself of Caribbean origin, lived in the street where the Temple is located and had found a ready welcome and acceptance.

At the Temple there are large gatherings for the Hindu festivals. The President and the committee members, as well as the priest, Pandit Ramsaran Sankar, are always pleased when guests from other faiths are present. And this openness is not confined to events at the Temple. When Rabbi James Baaden at South London Liberal Synagogue arranged the second of his multi faith concerts, known as *Faithsounds*, the chosen date was 7 July 2005. The bombings in London that day forced a postponement until the October, and the programme then included Hindu songs performed in the Synagogue by Bhisham Dindayal, the then President of the Caribbean Hindu Society, and his wife Radikha.

The openness of the Temple is also evident in its participation in school visit programmes in the London Borough of Lambeth. Here Ganesh's contribution has been much appreciated. He receives and teaches the children and answers questions with great clarity, often anticipating the (stereotypical) questions. By all accounts, the same qualities came to the fore when forty-five local teachers met at the Temple after school for Inset training, most of them visiting a Hindu temple for the first time.

An appreciation of the role of the Caribbean Hindu Society and its Temple, rooted in the history of Guyana in particular, gives us a clearer picture of the context from which Ganesh Lall is coming. But within that context Ganesh often takes a very independent line. Letters of his that have been published in *The Times* give an insight into his particular stance. In one letter he comments on a decision to remove a cross from the Torbay Council chapel. This had been done on the grounds that we live in a diverse, multi faith society and that the council had a duty to cater for everyone. Ganesh wrote: 'As a Hindu, I object to such action being taken in my name. It is offensive to the majority Christian community. Far from catering for everyone, it serves only to create disharmony in the community.' On another occasion his letter made a robust comment, not about arranged marriages as such, but about the high incidence of such marriages involving overseas partners:

This prevents successful integration, lends itself to abuse, such as sham marriages, inhibits genuine choice – and is an insult to members of the Asian community who are born here. The beneficiaries are the self-styled religious Asian leaders, who have much to gain by preserving an increasingly outmoded system in the name of religion and culture.

The South London Inter Faith Group

The South London Inter Faith Group has been one of the organisations where Ganesh Lall has made a very important contribution, serving on its committee and giving time and effort to further its aims. His approach is typical of the organisation itself. Here is how it presented itself at the time of its twenty-fifth anniversary in 2006:

- 25 years committed to greater understanding among people of faith
- We live in South London
- We want to learn about each other's religions
- We like to meet new friends of faith locally
- We like to visit places of prayer and worship
- We hope to encourage mutual understanding of the teachings, traditions and practices among the faith communities of South London
- We respect each other's religion and conversion is no part of our aim

South London Inter Faith Group was founded in 1981 by Brian Pearce and Ivor Smith Cameron. It was one of the first inter faith organisations in London, though preceded by six years by Wandsworth and Merton Inter Faith Group, with which it amalgamated in 1991. In 1981 there were still only about ten local inter faith groups in the UK. This number grew steadily to around 100 in 2001, and has since then grown more quickly. The 2007 edition of the very useful directory of inter faith organisations published by the Inter Faith Network for the United Kingdom gives details of 217 local inter faith groups.

South London Inter Faith Group (SLIFG) is based on individual membership, with typically around 250 members. There are other kinds of inter faith organisation, but SLIFG wants to continue to play its part as an independent, individual membership body. South London is a big place and, with the growing numbers of inter faith groups, many of its members are also active in more locally focused groups.

SLIFG has meetings at different places in South London about six times a year, plus an annual all-day inter faith walk, visiting five or six faith communities in their places of worship, usually in collaboration with a more local multi faith group. The events include speakers, discussion, dance, film, and visits to faith communities and places of worship. There is an effort to tackle important topical issues from a multi faith perspective. Social occasions and sharing food together are very important.

SLIFG has members in all twelve of the Greater London boroughs south of the River Thames, as well as some members who live outside the South London area. The committee currently includes Baha'i, Buddhist, Christian, Hindu, Jewish, Muslim and Sikh members.

In 2006, two studies were commissioned as part of a twenty-fifth anniversary review of the role of South London Inter Faith Group. Two reports were prepared: *Improved Understanding of South London's Multi Faith Situation* by Sarah Thorley, and *An Evaluation of Different Models of Inter Faith Activity* by Siriol Davies. These studies, funded by the Faith Communities Capacity Building Fund, are enabling SLIFG to discern its proper role alongside the more than 20 local inter faith organisations that are now active across South London.

For a few years the South London Inter Faith Group saw rather less of Ganesh than we had become accustomed to. He had become a student on a Study of Religions degree course at London University's School of Oriental and African Studies. Ganesh's academic success brought great pleasure to everyone, and there was a special celebration at the Caribbean Hindu Society.

Ganesh soon returned to a very full involvement with inter faith activities. He gave tremendous support to the *Understanding Islam* course which Dr Chris Hewer from St Ethelburga's Centre ran at All Saints' Church Battersea for ten weeks at the beginning of 2007. Around 40 people attended, and it was typical of Ganesh that he cooked lunch for everyone on the occasion of the first meeting. As a sequel, Pandit Sankar of the Caribbean Hindu Society led three sessions called *Introducing Hinduism* in the summer of 2007.

Ongoing inter faith training for Anglicans

Going back to the story of training in the Diocese of Southwark, it was not long after the inter faith module was introduced to the Diocesan Certificate in Christian Discipleship that a further step was taken to add inter faith content to diocesan training courses. The Ordained Local Ministry Training Scheme wanted to enhance its inter faith training and looked to the Diocesan Inter Faith Group for assistance. The requirement was for visits to a synagogue, a mosque or Islamic centre, and a place of worship of one other faith community, spread over an academic term, topped and tailed by an introductory session and a review session. Paul Collier and I set up this module in the autumn term of 2002. This seemed to work well, but there was a change the following year when the OLM inter faith training module became also a module of the Diocesan Summer School. After a few more years the OLM course decided to set up additional inter faith training for its students; and the Summer School module, with its 'three visits plus two sessions' format, has continued to be offered each year to all who have an interest.

On two occasions the Caribbean Hindu Society, through Ganesh's good offices, has hosted one of the Summer School visits. The first such visit was during an ordinary Friday evening at the Temple, when there is regularly a small gathering to offer devotions through music, song, and scripture reading. The next year the visit took place on the occasion of Guru Purnima, one of the Temple's festivals. This gave an excellent opportunity to experience the liturgy, led by the priest, and also the hospitality and strong communal life of the Temple.

Another strand of development in diocesan training has concerned lay ministers. After discussion with the training staff, it was decided to offer the same 'three visits plus two sessions' format to newly commissioned Southwark Pastoral Auxiliaries (SPAs) and soon-to-be-licensed Readers in September 2005. There was a good response and the pattern was repeated in 2006 and 2007.

Among the various diocesan training courses, there is a difference of opinion about the Certificate in Biblical and Theological Studies. In this course the doctrine tutors discuss the view of Jesus in other faiths as a way of illuminating Christian understanding, and some feel that it should go no further in an inter faith direction. Others, though, are convinced that it is of the essence of Christian theology today that it should examine its exclusivist tendencies in the light of the more informed appreciation of other faiths that Christians are gaining with the help of friends like Ganesh Lall. This debate will no doubt continue.

Face to face encounter

Visits to the places of worship of other faiths, with some time to reflect together about the shared experiences, have proved a valuable tool in the provision of inter faith training; but alongside such visits the 'face to face encounter with someone of another faith' offers further advantages. Sessions where between five and twenty Anglicans sit with a guest from another faith for 60–90 minutes have transformed the outlook of many of the participants. Along with Ganesh, both Rabbi James Baaden of the South London Liberal Synagogue and Ebrahim Rashid of the Hyderi Islamic Centre have given their time and skills unstintingly to such occasions.

As I said at the outset, the first time I sat in on a session for which Ganesh was the 'someone from another faith', the learning that was possible made a deep impression on me. Ganesh's affirmation of the oneness of God in Hindu understanding later came across to me in a powerful experiential way when Pandit Sankar was praying before one of the Introducing Hinduism sessions at All Saints' Church. It just felt so obvious that he was addressing prayer to the one God. Ganesh's statement that 'Hinduism' is a western construct and that it would be more accurate to refer to 'the religious tradition of India' led us to understand that, not being a 'faith', Indian religious tradition has no creeds and no commandments; that conversion is an inconceivable notion (all the Christians listening seemed deeply struck by this); and that the whole truth is never known, so the differing spiritual journeys of others deserve deep respect. Also challenging to Christians was Ganesh's approach to historicity. 'We don't ask', he said, 'whether Jesus or Krishna or Buddha was *really* here on earth. It is the message which matters.'

Ganesh's particular background, like that of many in his community, includes a close association with Christianity through schools and churches. He himself attended a Christian school in Guyana, and when he first came to Britain there were no temples so he went to church. So when a point is being made about an aspect of Indian religious tradition, you may well hear a text from the Gospels being quoted by way of illustration.

From the success of Ganesh's sessions, Sarah Thorley developed useful guidelines for such occasions, to assist others in taking on the role that she had fulfilled as 'enabler'. There is a suggested timetable, and advice that the guest of another faith should leave plenty of time for questions and discussion and speak as personally as he or she feels able to. Participants are encouraged to come with an open mind and to have visited a Hindu temple beforehand if possible.

When Ganesh was the guest the creation of a good atmosphere was assisted by recorded music (Hindu bhajans), a reading from the Upanishads, books, artefacts and food (samosas and Indian sweets). Of course, depending on the guest, and depending on the faith to which the guest belonged, the details of the arrangements would vary. On occasions when Ebrahim Rashid and Imam Shakeel Begg led very fruitful evenings, their brief opening recitations of verses from the Holy Qur'an immediately communicated a great deal and helped to create a good atmosphere.

The changing scene

After six or more years' experience of the kind of inter faith educational programmes mentioned in this chapter, there is a need to be alert to changed approaches that may be required as time goes on. The diocesan context has meanwhile changed substantially. The structures have been revamped and the inter faith element is now an Inter Faith Relationships Sub-group of a Mission Group, with an emphasis primarily on an agenda called Presence and Engagement, about the role of Church of England parishes in multi faith areas. Meanwhile the Discipleship Certificate has faded away and Ordained Local Ministry has been dropped as a separate stream of ministry. The Summer School and Reader–SPA modules are now organised by the South London Inter Faith Group. Previously 'Christianity in Multi Faith Britain', the title now is 'Inter Faith Relationships in Britain Today'. One idea for the future is to pilot a short training course of this type designed to serve the needs of people drawn from various faith communities in an area, and a step towards this has been to relax the prescription that the three visits should be to a synagogue, a mosque or Islamic centre, and one other. For example, a very enthusiastic Reader–SPA course led by Jeanette McLaren in September 2007 visited a Buddhist centre, a Hindu temple (the Caribbean Hindu Society again) and a Sikh gurdwara. Meanwhile, there is a pool of Christians keen to take advantage of more substantial inter faith educational opportunities. The ten-session *Understanding Islam* course, for example, is attracting considerable interest, running during the early part of 2008 in at least five parallel series at different locations in South London.

Reflecting on all this, it appears that inter faith training for Anglicans in South London has not had the benefit of a fully resourced, sustained or consistent diocesan strategy. This is a result, I suspect, of the considerable range of views that exists within Anglican theology about the nature of inter faith relationships. Despite these limitations, significant numbers have been enabled to benefit from the training opportunities on offer, and a growing grassroots movement is leading more and more parishes, deaneries and ecumenical groupings to set up their own inter faith programmes. Whatever the details of the future shape might be, it is wonderful to feel a confidence that Ganesh and others like him will continue to give generously of themselves and their time to work for 'greater understanding among people of faith'.

Response by Ganesh Lall

Three incidents have shaped my attitudes to religion as a Hindu, and prepared the way for me to play my part in the educational programmes that Alan Gadd has described.

On the occasion of the marriage of an elder cousin, my father drew a *mandala*, a sacred circle on the ground within the ceremonial space under the *maro*, a temporary tent built for the celebration. Inside the circle he wrote with yellow-coloured rice a sacred Sanskrit verse. Under it he wrote a quotation from Matthew 19.6: 'What God hath joined together, let no man put asunder.'

The second incident occurred when I was approaching my teens. Father Kidd, a corpulent and amiable Yorkshireman, came to visit my eldest uncle, head of our Hindu joint family of four brothers and their families. He remarked how happy he was that the children, thirteen in all, were attending Sunday school regularly and doing so well. He then politely suggested that maybe it was time for us to be baptised. My uncle, just about able to contain his rage, stood up and quite courteously gave Father Kidd a short lesson in Hinduism. 'We seek knowledge wherever it can be found,' he said, 'but we remain Hindus.' We continued to attend Sunday school and Father Kidd was our honoured guest at a farewell dinner when his tour of duty ended.

The third related to the death-bed request of an elderly uncle who had married a Christian lady. He had been baptised and changed his name from Kissoon to Joseph. My aunt pre-deceased him. A few years later as he lay dying he sent for me as his closest relative. He asked to be cremated according to the Hindu rites. When I expressed mild surprise, he confessed to me that in all the years since his marriage he had never turned his back on his ancestral religion.

My father had never heard of inter faith dialogue. He didn't engage in it: he lived it. For him it was a fact of life. Father Kidd was engaged in the battle for human souls. His agenda had no place to accommodate Hinduism. Christianity for him had an exclusive access to truth, and this went against the Hindu teaching that there are aspects of truth present in every great religion. This was exemplified by Mahatma Gandhi, whose words head this chapter.

My uncle, for whatever reason, was baptised as a Christian; but his new faith did not supersede or replace his old one. It simply became another layer of spiritual experience. Conversion goes against the spirit of Hinduism. Unethical pressure to convert is anathema to a Hindu and can be a source of conflict and disharmony in Hindu society. Hindus respect others and expect others to respect them in return. Proselytisation and mutual respect are incompatible.

As a Hindu, I have an abiding love of Jesus and his teachings. I have the deepest respect for all religions, but with a special place for Christianity. As an immigrant I consider myself extremely fortunate to be living in the UK, which I regard as a predominantly Christian country. This is reflected in the people and their laws, their values, and their way of life. My life here has been an enriching experience.

These three experiences have taught me that it is not enough to talk inter faith. All religions must go further. They must interact and intermingle. We must meet with people of other faiths until it becomes such a natural act that it would cease to be a meeting of religions: it would be a fellowship of like minds united in a common purpose.

Further reading

David Dabydeen and Brinsley Samaroo (eds), 1987/2006, *India in the Caribbean*, Hertford: Hansib Publications.

Siriol Davies, 2007, *An Evaluation of Different Models of Inter Faith Activity*, London: South London Inter Faith Group: available from South London Inter Faith Group, 24 Holmewood Gardens, London SW2 3RS.

Presence and Engagement: The churches' task in a multi faith society, 2005, GS 1577, London: The General Synod of the Church of England.

Sarah Thorley, 2007, *Improved Understanding of South London's Multi Faith Situation*, London: South London Inter Faith Group: available from South London Inter Faith Group, 24 Holmewood Gardens, London SW2 3RS.

Note

1 www.gandhiserve.org/cwmg/VOL023.PDF, p. 215.

8 Women Together

A women's group in South London

MAUREEN MULLALLY

with a response by Linda de Lange

Bear with one another and, if anyone has a complaint against another, forgive each other; just as the Lord has forgiven you, so you also must forgive. Above all, clothe yourselves with love, which binds everything together in perfect harmony.

Colossians 3.13–14

Righteous people of all nations have a share in the world to come.

Babylonian Talmud[1]

It was perhaps with a certain curiosity mixed with some trepidation that a few parishioners of St Joseph's Catholic Church in Bromley arrived at the Muslim mosque in Lewisham one dark evening. None of us had actually visited a mosque before, except perhaps as tourists in some Islamic country. Now we were going to share in prayer with our brothers and sisters of the Muslim faith, the Jewish faith, and other Christian denominations.

The mosque was not particularly easy to find, situated as it was in the middle of shops on a busy bus route, still crowded with home-going traffic. For those of us who knew very little about the Muslim faith, myself included, the first surprise was the separate entrances for men and women. We were to be segregated for the duration of the visit. Facing us on arrival, inside the women's entrance, were shelves divided into cubbyholes for our shoes. Footwear must be removed on entry to a mosque as a sign of respect. Then we women had to climb a steep flight of stairs to a room above the main body of the mosque where the men were, together with their Imam. Of course, we had already covered our heads.

Upstairs we found comfortable seating and the warmest possible welcome from the women who were waiting for us. We were screened off from the lower part of the mosque, but were told it was permissible to peep down on the men who were to take part in the service. Several of them were accompanied by male children, some very small indeed, all very well behaved; it was apparent that even the youngest appreciated the solemnity of what they had come to do.

When the prayers began, the Muslim ladies unselfconsciously prostrated themselves on the floor to join in. There was an impressive atmosphere of reverence and quiet attention. We prayed with them silently in our own words.

Altogether, there were about twenty of us, members of the three faiths. We were soon chatting away, like most women when they get together, introducing ourselves to one another and thoroughly appreciating the delicious buffet that had been prepared for us.

The Three Faiths Forum was instituted in 1997 to encourage friendship, goodwill and understanding among people of the three Abrahamic faiths, in the UK and elsewhere. It would support and promote public recognition of groups where people of the Muslim, Christian and Jewish faiths meet and share common interests and experiences. It encourages respect for religious differences between the three faiths on a basis of equality and exploration, enjoying those differences where appropriate. It also aims to promote the training of ministers of religion of the three faiths in their common roots, understanding of their differences, and mutual respect on an equal standing. The recognition of our differences was an important aspect of our meeting that evening in Lewisham. Even so, there were some, to me, surprising manifestations of Muslim belief in the large pictures of Jesus and his mother Mary to be seen on the walls of the room where we were. It was intriguing and encouraging to discover that Muslims regard Jesus as a great prophet and venerate the Blessed Virgin for having given birth to him.

As questions and explanations led to a lively debate, there were a few among us who were clearly finding it difficult to accept what our Muslim sisters were telling us about the necessity for them to be segregated from men. They were serenely confident that this did not mean that they had a lesser place in their families or their faith. In the Muslim home, they told us, the wife and mother holds unchallenged sway over her family. They had no problem about not sharing meetings with men: they told us that they would not like to express opinions in public in the company of men, and they did not feel this to be a deprivation. A couple of the participants wondered whether, in that case, it would be possible for us to meet them again other than in the mosque. We were all enjoying sharing information about our religions and about our children and grandchildren. We had so much in common there: mothers and grandmothers share a language that overcomes all barriers. Moreover, we were there, after all, to gain more understanding of the faith of others, not to criticise aspects with which we might not find ourselves in agreement. Very soon the suggestion was made that we should have separate meetings for women hosted by members of each faith in turn. The Christian and Jewish ladies could continue to attend the general meetings of the Forum in addition to these proposed get-togethers. Someone kindly offered to have a tea party in her own home and a date was agreed.

And that is how it all began. The meetings have been taking place at intervals of six or eight weeks ever since. We have met in our homes, and most recently the meetings have been generously hosted by Sister Marie-Edel at Holy Trinity Convent in Bromley, a venue that affords plenty of space for everyone who wishes to come. Members of the group bring plates of food, often typical of the cuisine of their own culture, and it has to be said that the Jewish and Muslim dishes tend to be more popular than the more bland 'Christian' contributions.

We say a simple prayer to begin the meeting. After that the conversation never flags. We are all so delighted to see one another again that we usually have to be called to order so that exploration of the topic for the afternoon can begin. At an early stage we planned to embroider a cloth which was to have all of our initials, together with representations of emblems of the three faiths. Life being as busy as it is, it has to be confessed that the task of embroidery has not proceeded as quickly as we might have hoped, but a start has been made and when, eventually, it has been completed, it will make a treasured souvenir of our joint efforts. Every meeting has a theme which is addressed by a member of each faith. These have included 'The Meaning of Life', 'Weddings', 'Funerals', 'What We Believe', 'Prayer', and 'The

Meaning of Charity'. Each topic brings us fascinating insights into the beliefs and customs that we share and the ways in which we are different. On one occasion one of our Jewish members brought a copy of a study tenach (or Hebrew Bible, which is approximately the same as the writings which Christians know as the Old Testament), and we were able to see for ourselves how it is set out: the main text on the middle of each page, with the interpretations of various scholars in the margins. The Muslim Qur'an and the Christian Bible have also been discussed.

Interest in the presentations is keen and people are not afraid to disagree or put another point of view. We have all learned such a lot over the months and have become real friends. A highlight of a tea party at my home was that Amatullah, one of the Muslim young women, arrived with her new baby. Everyone wanted to exclaim over how beautiful she was, and we were allowed to give her a cuddle. We are all constantly being surprised, which is good for us. For example, although I already had many Jewish friends, I did not realise that, for some members of the Jewish faith at any rate, it is offensive to hear the name of God spoken. This does not just apply to a blasphemous use of the name, which would be objectionable to any member of the three religions. Orthodox Jews do not utter the name of God, even with respect. We are so confident of our own conventions of speech that we take for granted that they must be acceptable to every hearer. My Jewish friends had obviously been too polite in the past ever to point out my tactlessness.

We have managed to survive a good deal of pain. One meeting was held shortly after the London bombings in July 2005. Our Muslim members were describing to us how difficult things were for them, as they were identifiable as Muslims by their dress in the street, and all too conscious that they were being regarded with suspicion and condemnation by passers-by. The true Muslim faith does not approve or condone violence but, especially at that time, the generality of the population, understandably shocked and grieving, were prepared to blame all Muslims for the evil perpetrated by the suicide bombers, and they made their feelings quite clear.

The situation in the Middle East seems to have deteriorated progressively since our group was formed, but I have never heard a Jewish or Muslim member make any comment that could be hurtful to another. We feel it is an achievement that tragic world events have not impacted unfavourably on the mutual understanding that has been forged between us. Not everyone can attend every meeting and numbers vary, but the warmth and affection that have grown among us are a tribute to our determination that understanding should overcome prejudice.

If we have a regret then it must be that we have so few young members, especially those belonging to the Christian and Jewish faiths. It is, of course, difficult for younger women to find time to come to meetings like this – mothers of families, career women, or those struggling to combine the two roles as so many do. But we know that we must recruit the younger generation, particularly as the majority of the Muslims who come are young parents.

Ours is a very small group, but if we are ever to achieve mutual tolerance and understanding between the three great Abrahamic faiths then it is from initiatives like ours that this could grow. Maybe it wasn't such a bad thing that the Muslim women had to be segregated.

Response by Linda de Lange

As a Progressive Jew I first became involved in the Lewisham and Bromley branch of the Three Faiths Forum just after it was set up some four years ago.

My memory of my first meetings is that we sat and discussed things in largish groups in which the goodwill was already there but little friendship or understanding was being fostered. However, fairly quickly the meetings evolved into smaller discussion groups all talking about the same subject. This format tended to work much better as it allowed greater understanding and friendship to develop. This might be because smaller groups make it easier for everyone to join in: they leave more time and space for people to get to know each other.

I also think that the discussions have become more considered and tactful. It's one thing to announce your views as if they were infallible to a large group. It's much harder to do this when you can see the puzzlement or pain those views cause reflected in the eyes of people sitting close to you. In smaller groups other people are also more likely to ask you to explain exactly what you mean without it sounding like a direct challenge.

Recently I was at one of our most poorly attended meetings

(only nine of us turned up), yet I think it was actually one of the best. We managed to offend each other, work out what was offensive, explain that to each other, and then move on to greater understanding. I doubt if that could have been done in a large group.

In this type of discussion I am forced to clarify my own views and really think about what I believe rather than just giving a stock answer. In some ways this is probably easier for me as a Progressive Jew as questioning, doubt and multiplicity of views sit very comfortably within the framework of Progressive Judaism. However, by listening to others I have begun to realise that questioning and doubt can seem like hypocrisy to some people, and I have been forced to question what lies at the heart of my own beliefs. This has helped me to strengthen my understanding of my own religion.

I have found that this happens more easily in the women's group meetings, which tend to be even smaller and friendlier. The women's group was set up, as Maureen says, because the Muslim sisters felt unable to take part in the larger mixed-sex groups. While part of me felt that I didn't want to be segregated, I was also very keen that it should be possible for Muslim women to take part in inter faith work. In the event I have found it to be very enjoyable, and I have met women there whom I would now count as friends. I believe that such friendship is an important aspect of inter faith work. While it is good to understand the tenets of another's religion, it is even better to have someone tell you that they always thought Jews were uncaring, rich and insular, but that now they know they are not. Similarly, I now know that the face behind the veil can belong to an intelligent, independently minded woman rather than the subjugated drudge of stereotype. Furthermore, I have discovered that not all Christians feel that they have a direct line to God, and that they too struggle to understand how they should behave when faced with life's challenges.

We have also tried to foster friendship and understanding by engaging in social activities. We have had some meetings in the park where members could bring their children and simply enjoy themselves; and I have recently hosted an inter faith picnic in my garden. Also recently twelve of us – women and men – got together to wash cars to raise money for Darfur (we raised over £200 in three hours). Although I was the only woman car washer I was accepted as one of the 'lads' and in four mixed faith groups we knocked on doors and managed to persuade some fairly bemused people that we were a good cause and that they had very dirty cars. I would very much like to do more of this kind of thing. It was very enjoyable as we all joked around a lot, it allowed others to see a group of religious people working together to do something practical to help others, and dialogue took place between the suds and the laughs.

However, while I feel I have learnt a lot from the views of others and have had some very enjoyable times, as a Jew I find that there are particular issues that I have to deal with when engaging in inter faith dialogue. For instance, Jews on the whole are more comfortable talking about ethical issues than theological ones. Partly this is because we have a long history of having to justify our religion to others. Until very recently Jews had always been a minority within the various countries in which they resided. The difficult history we have endured has made us feel that any theological discussion is meant to make us feel that our religion has been superseded by others. I do not mean here that others within the group have tried to make that point (well, only very occasionally, and they have usually been reprimanded by one of their own). Rather, this is one of the inner demons a Jew engaging in inter faith dialogue has to deal with.

There is another reason which may seem strange to non-Jews. A Jew's relationship with God is seen as something personal and private, and people talking about their own personal relationship with God can seem quite shocking, almost rude. This is probably related to Jewish wariness of evangelism. Both Muslims and Christians seek to spread their religion, and while I understand the underlying theological reasons for this it can sometimes make me feel uncomfortable and at times suspicious. I do appreciate that the members of the group try very hard not to evangelise, but as a Jew I am very wary of things like group prayer. Maureen mentions group prayer at the beginning of the meetings. However, although I have attended almost all of the general and women's meetings, I myself have never taken part in a group prayer.

I know that the issues I have outlined above lie at the heart of my own community's discomfort with inter faith work, and at times I have found it difficult to get others involved. This is made even harder because we are a very small community and we are always being asked to give talks to local schools and churches and to join in various inter faith initiatives. The few people who are interested in inter faith work can quite quickly find themselves swamped with requests to explain the Jewish viewpoint to others, and this can make them feel guilty that they are not doing more to support their own community.

However, I feel that this work is of vital importance. We live in uncertain times when many see religious difference as lying at the heart of conflict. Personally, I believe that most of these conflicts are based on various underlying causes, few of which have anything directly to do with religion. Nevertheless, when people draw themselves into religious groups to fight their cause then it can become very dangerous. So I hope that inter faith engagement can help us to recognise our shared values and accept our differences, and in the process to find resolution for conflict. Our group has deliberately concentrated on the first of the Three Faiths Forum's aims, which is to seek to foster goodwill, understanding and friendship by providing situations where everyone is able to speak. This has meant that we have never done anything very glamorous, and we have held no town hall receptions or inter faith services, for example. But we have smiled and shared, and in doing so I hope that we have helped a little to create a space for dialogue where differences can be accepted if not resolved.

Note

1 According to www.newworldencyclopedia.org/entry/Noahide_ Laws, the reference is Talmud, Sanhedrin 105a, but in the version at www.come-and-hear.com/sanhedrin/sanhedrin_105.html the point is a more negative one: i.e. that Gentiles are not necessarily denied the world to come. A similarly worded text, 'the pious of all nations have a portion in the world to come', appears at Tractate Abodah Zarah 10, quoting Tosef. San. XIII: www.come-and-hear.com/zarah/zarah_10. html.

9 Serving the Community Together

A Christian teaching in a Muslim Centre

HELEN BAILEY

with a response by Hanan Kasmi

Happy are those who find wisdom, and those who get understanding, for her income is better than silver, and her revenue
better than gold.

Proverbs 3.13–14

He gives wisdom to whom he will, and he that receives the gift
of wisdom is rich indeed. But none except men of sense bear
this in mind.

The Holy Qur'an, Sura 2.269[1]

The background and the beginning

'Helen, I've no idea what your plans are, but . . .' It was my friend
Sarah Thorley, on the line from London. I was at my parents'
home in Cheshire and this early morning conversation was to
call me back down south to the city I had left over a year earlier
to go to live and work in the Middle East.

I had not long returned from Lebanon where I had been living
out what I felt very much to be 'my mission' at the time: to work
with the poorest and most marginalised, particularly the
Palestinian refugees. I had taught English to Shi'a Muslim
youngsters denied schooling, and trained refugee women
kindergarten teachers. My Arabic had improved and I had learnt
a lot about the fascinating spectrum of Christianity and Islam
across the region. Having been hooked on the Middle East
since my first visit to the Holy Land in 1990, I was fulfilled. Now
I was back in the UK with no fixed plans. I felt I should continue

teaching rather than go back to desk-based aid work as I had been doing for Christian Aid before I went away. But what was open to me and where? I was at a crossroads in my life.

'Southwark Muslim Women's Association are absolutely desperate for an English teacher.' This sounded interesting. My excitement mounted as Sarah continued speaking. They knew I had been teaching Muslim children and were keen to talk to me. I could picture the Centre: a warm and friendly place, a bright building with lots going on. South London Inter Faith Group had visited it as part of their annual inter faith walk in 2001 and I had been impressed.

Beliefs and Britain

'The person to talk to is Hanan.' And so began a partnership and a friendship that was to deepen during the months that followed. Hanan was the manager of the supplementary education project and my new boss. She smiled warmly as she strode purposefully towards me with hand outstretched to grasp mine. I was shocked that my reaction was one of slight surprise that she was wearing the hijab. Was it something to do with us being in England, with her being young, an educated professional, very much a British Muslim? Certainly it was everything to do with me and my expectations.

During our time together I learnt a lot from Hanan and my respect for her grew. From a family of Moroccan origin and brought up in Lewisham, she is as happy speaking Arabic as she is English. With her background in anti-discrimination and rights-based work she taught me a great deal about working with and educating children. Hanan respected our pupils and treated them as individuals – while being strict on discipline and taking no nonsense. Above all, though, she really loved them and had their highest welfare at heart. Of immense integrity and a woman of her word, she is probably the most highly organised person I have ever worked with. *Inshallah* (God willing), when uttered by Hanan, struck me as not just the oft-used formula by Muslims for some vague future possibility, but an expression of hopeful trust in God. She is sincere about her faith: it informs her values and she expresses it in her actions.

I had developed an interest in and some understanding of Islam initially through my experiences of Muslim people and practices in the Middle East, Morocco, East Africa and Pakistan; and now it was all, in a way, coming to me. I was encountering Islam first hand within my own culture. Morocco, Algeria, Pakistan, Bangladesh, Eritrea, Somalia and Turkey are the origins of many of the members of Southwark Muslim Women's Association. Although I had visited a number of London mosques and met Sunni and Shi'a Muslims in different contexts through the South London Inter Faith Group, it was working on a daily basis in a Muslim-run centre that meant I was to be challenged, encouraged, inspired, but sometimes frustrated and disappointed too. In addition, my views and knowledge of Islam were somewhat to change and broaden. Working in that environment made me extremely aware of myself: how I acted, what I said, and even, sometimes, what I wore. I was a representative of my faith, although of course I was not hired because of it (and didn't really speak too much of it). Most important was that as staff we shared the Centre's ethos of care for its community, upheld its positive values, and did a professional job.

From an ecumenical church background and with, I think, a pretty open heart and mind, I nevertheless struggle with what I sometimes feel to be the tension of wanting to explore my own faith and roots while remaining open to exploring others; but I have come to know that learning about another faith can sincerely enrich and deepen our own. When I discussed this chapter with my father, a retired Anglican priest, he remarked that his many years of experience in ecumenical co-operation had both affirmed his own beliefs and led him to a deeper respect for those of other denominations. I can identify very much with that. But I am probably jumping ahead. What I did know at the time was that God had opened the doors for me in Lebanon the previous year, so perhaps in some way I was uniquely placed to take on this new role.

The community and the Centre

The Southwark Muslim Women's Association (SMWA) is in a regenerated area of Peckham on Bellenden Road. Peckham is not known for its good news, more for its social ills. The schoolboy Damilola Taylor was murdered there near his own doorstep by children around his own age. Peckham is the poorest and most disadvantaged part of the borough of Southwark. It also has the most young people. Its largest community is black and nearly 40 per cent of its population were born outside the UK. The borough itself is one of the most religiously diverse in the country. Muslims make up 10 per cent of Peckham's population, higher than the average for London, and they form the largest religious community in the area after Christians. The Muslim community in Southwark includes many people on low incomes and state benefits, often living in overcrowded conditions. One third of them are black African.

SMWA was established nearly 30 years ago to serve the local Muslim community, 'to provide the Muslim women of Southwark with the skills, confidence and qualifications to enable them to enrich their lives within our Muslim traditions'.[2] It also aims 'to counter disadvantages and discrimination faced by Muslim communities in Southwark with a special emphasis on meeting the needs of women, children and elders'.[3] Men are not necessarily excluded.

Amid many celebrations, the Association won the Muslim News Award for Community Development, as reported in the *Muslim News* citation of 23 March 2005:

> SMWA is celebrating its silver jubilee. This family centre in south east London offers education, activities, youth projects and social events for Muslim women and their families. Many women appreciate the friendly atmosphere at SMWA and the crèche facilities ensure they are free to enjoy health and fitness classes, dress-making, language lessons and much more.

Involved with some 500 member families from around the globe, over the years the Association has developed in response to social and political changes and the needs of its community, particularly so as to overcome the isolation and exclusion many have experienced since 9/11. The Centre, the entire ground floor of a refurbished old school building, is a place of safety and support. Members come with many challenges in their lives, often related to living in a different culture. As Islam is central to the culture of all of them, they can feel free at SMWA to observe – and celebrate – the customs and traditions of their faith without restriction or embarrassment. This is particularly important for the women. Many of them have few other social activities and, although learning is important to them, meeting each other socially is often even more so.

SMWA extends beyond its base. I had first encountered them on an inter faith walk when the entire Centre had been given over to an excellent exhibition about Islam around the world. Through a range of events and activities each year, including festival celebrations, the Association promotes Muslim culture and traditions to a wider community, including other faith groups and local schools. Not long after our first term started, the Centre ran an exhibition of Muslim arts, crafts and culture for Black History Month. Other annual events that took place during my time there included International Women's Day activities and a Ramadan exhibition at the nearby Horniman Museum. SMWA is committed to working with those of other faiths and communities in Southwark and beyond, and is keen to contribute to creating a community of respect and understanding of others in society. It has achieved a reputation as a model for community organisations and shares good practice with other boroughs.

Meeting the children

I had taught the poorest and most disadvantaged in Beirut's notorious southern suburbs and in the sadly infamous Shatila refugee camp, but now I was to be teaching Peckham schoolchildren. Peckham pupils consistently underperform those in the rest of the borough and around the UK at all stages in the core subjects of English, maths, IT (information technology) and science.[4] So, through Saturday school and after-school classes, local children came to improve their grades and their confidence. In addition some attended Arabic or Urdu mother-tongue classes. They also studied arts and crafts. Islam values education highly and promotes a holistic approach to it, and Islamic ethics are valued for their positive influence on young Muslims in education. Coming from families who, in the main, cared about their children's educational achievements, most of our children wanted to do well. Some had high aspirations: to be a barrister, a doctor, or an accountant. They struggled, though. Even those from families rooted in sound, faith-based values faced a barrage of pressures and influences, often confusing, undermining, and even overwhelming, with few black role models aside from pop stars and sports personalities. The supplementary school project was all about them fulfilling potential, building confidence and self-esteem, and developing respect for self and others. It was also about promoting their development in all ways and preparing them for citizenship and for life.

'Who's heard of Islamophobia?' Hanan was inducting us tutors before we started teaching. In mainstream education Muslims in the UK may face discrimination towards their faith, which can contribute to poor performance at school. So we were encouraged to consider strategies and responses to this within the classroom and through the curriculum that we were to teach. We were working in an environment that positively valued different cultural traditions.

Another key issue for Muslim pupils is language. Poor proficiency in English can affect educational attainment, and within the home many UK Muslim children speak a language other than English. So I had my work cut out.

Day one. After a full day at school, children from across the borough and beyond, aged 7–15, started to arrive at the Centre. Black and white, small and bigger, male and female (some veiled, some not), some very intelligent, some very challenged, and not all Muslim. I was introduced to Bradley, an independent-minded and enthusiastic eight-year-old with origins in Ivory Coast, and a proud Christian. Bradley's father's deep and personal faith was clearly influencing his son in positive ways. This being the third year of the supplementary school project, its benefits had spread outside the Muslim community. Hanan had good contacts with the schools in the area as well as with the children's parents.

Meeting the women

I had been in my job less than a week when I was called into the director's office. There was a waiting list of women desperate to learn English: could I take on a class? And so I became a tutor of English to Speakers of Other Languages (ESOL). God had now provided me with enough work and enough money.

Adult education remains at the core of the Association's work. It's all about improving confidence, gaining skills and qualifications, and developing employability. Muslim women face a number of barriers to employment, of which the lack of affordable and culturally appropriate childcare is a major factor. So SMWA has a crèche. Only a third of Muslim women in London aged twenty-five or over are doing any kind of paid work, and more than that number look after the home.[5] On completing their courses many of SMWA's students show an interest in further study to improve their skills, although a quarter of these are unwilling to study anywhere other than at the Centre. I had another uphill task.

Characters and celebrations

We had many promising pupils and I encouraged them all to develop their imagination as much as possible and to read widely. Young Uzair was a challenge to teach, but with great imagination; he wrote well and one day came to class proudly clutching a book of poems in which he had had one published. Twelve-year-old Zaber captured special moments in his writing. During Ramadan we read some Muslim poetry from around the world and he was inspired to write this:

Oh Allah
Ramadan is here
That means Eid is near
Time to pray
We all say
Oh Allah
Ramadan is gone
And the fasting is done
Which means time to celebrate!
Oh Allah[6]

Although the name 'Allah' always commanded the utmost respect from our pupils, the same could not be said for the name or word 'God'. Bradley clearly believed we were talking about the same God when we spoke of Allah, and it always affected me when some of the children used the name 'God' in less than respectful ways. In one lesson with the younger children I challenged one of them to think about what they were saying. Thoughtful Nemata had remembered a previous discussion and repeated my own words then: you were not to speak of God in that way because 'God is special'. A lesson well learned, I thought.

Although we followed the national curriculum for all our

subjects and taught to planned schemes of work, during the Muslim holy month of Ramadan we changed the focus and the pace. Many children didn't come to classes at all and those who did, showed up tired and hungry after a full day at school. Although fasting is not obligatory for children, many of our pupils, even as young as eight, were keen to join in the family pattern in some way during the month. I was inspired by them and some days I fasted too. So every afternoon we had iftar (fast-breaking) – vital not only for the pupils but also for the staff. We were a good team and somehow it felt like a family. I devised a quiz which focused on the links of Islam to the other Abrahamic faiths, Judaism and Christianity, and which was a great success.

This is what Nabila and Isra wrote in the SMWA education newsletter (December 2003) about breaking the fast together:

> Before *iftar*, we lay the mats on the floor, place food on the mats and get ready. Everyone comes and joins us in a circle around the mats. We put the radio on to listen to the *Azan* (the call to prayer). We break our fast with dates. We think it is nice to have *iftar* together because it's interesting and we spend time talking about Islam and learn things that we didn't know before. We play quizzes on Islam. After that we pray *Maghrib namaz* (sunset prayer). We also have discussion sessions on Islam, and what kinds of things we get up to in school.

But by no means was it all so positive. Sometimes as teachers we were ignored and insulted and our authority questioned. Pupils bullied other pupils, and fights broke out. There was generally a disruptive pupil in every group. Some children even had possessions stolen, and some parents were at their wits' end with their own children. To my knowledge, though, there was never any discrimination on the basis of faith or lack of it. At all times Hanan was totally supportive of her team of tutors and had a rigorous policy about unacceptable behaviour. The pupils loved her as much as she loved them. Only one was ever excluded. Children from black, Asian and minority ethnic groups in London have been excluded from school in disproportionate numbers,[7] so the Centre policy was as far as possible not to contribute to that.

Cultures and challenges

And then there were the women. Nahida, a married woman from Algeria, was the keenest. Young, bright and beautiful, always made up and dressed up, she was in tears at the end of the year when a clash of appointments meant she missed sitting her final exam. But as an intelligent and fast learner I am sure she has since done well. During the year she started to wear a headscarf more often. It was interesting to see and hear the women from different cultures sharing experiences and practices. Arabic was generally their language of communication although some of the South Asian women did not understand it. I could probably follow more than they, although I generally kept that quiet.

The younger women, one after the other, kept getting pregnant, so that by the end of the course almost half of them were expecting. And then of course raising a family started to take priority, although those with children were able to leave them in the crèche while they attended class. Without the crèche facilities most of them would not have been able to study.

A very different young woman was twenty-three-year-old Ubah. Always dressed from head to toe in a black chador (full length robe), she removed her niqab or face veil in class, so we had a mild panic if one of the male staff ever walked in. She had lost a leg in Somalia and this obviously affected her ability to live a normal life, although she seemed to live a busy one between the home, the classroom and the mosque. She struggled in lessons, though, and with little formal education was at basic literacy level. My other students were way ahead. I had run out of ideas and strategies so I looked for help.

The solution lay largely with Aashaw, the mother of Uzair, our 'poet' pupil. Aashaw was the Association's vice-chair and had been involved for the last six years. Interested in becoming a teaching assistant, she was keen to volunteer a few hours a week to help the women. Ubah came alive with individual attention. Sometimes Aashaw helped her with basic tasks, at other times she freed me to work with Ubah myself. I was then able to encourage her to talk about her life and family and so develop materials related to her needs and interests. As a consequence Ubah began to show clear, if characteristically slow, progress and grow in confidence. When we were learning about shopping we went on a class trip to Rye Lane. I set the others some tasks and then accompanied Ubah to look for shoes and bags – I think a fairly rare opportunity for her. I learnt a lot about teaching ESOL to literacy students through this experience. My lack of experience in the classroom had contributed to some students leaving in the first term and I had taken it quite personally; but I learnt from that too and had decided by the end of the academic year that I wanted to continue teaching English to adults and that I was going to get fully qualified.

The other ESOL tutor was a Muslim man. It was a shame we weren't able to work more closely together because he was a more experienced teacher than I was. Although I was keen to learn and to share, it rarely happened. There wasn't a huge range of resources at the Centre, either, which meant that preparing lessons was a constant challenge. I struggled with feelings of inadequacy a lot of the time. The co-ordinator of the adult education programme was extremely busy juggling many tasks and I just had to get on with my own job. I worked extremely hard and was sad that my efforts were not ultimately reflected in better exam results for the students.

One of the other things I struggled with during the year was that part of my heart still lay in Lebanon. I only really settled down after a return visit to Beirut at Easter. I clearly remember the last lesson before we broke up. The women had just left, and as I looked around the room I felt a tremendous surge of love or something for them and finally felt sure I was in the right place. At that moment Hanan wandered in. We somehow got talking about God and the world and what we were doing in it; we agreed that we shared a worldview and wondered about those without some sort of belief structure. It was a connection and a recognition of something important shared.

Sometimes I ate lunch with the women and we brought food in and shared it. During Ramadan I ate discreetly alone or left the building, but no one minded anyway. They respected my customs as much as I respected theirs. This respect didn't always seem to extend to everyone at all times, though. Sometimes I heard moans about some people's lack of respect and lack of sense of responsibility, particularly towards their children. But I didn't complain, nor did it feel my place to do so, although I got frustrated at times.

In the lessons we didn't often discuss faith. I was a bit wary of getting into a theological argument that no one would win. But one day a discussion started. They liked to talk, those women. I was explaining about the meaning of Christmas, I think, and the debate got hot and the questions came. 'But do you really believe this about Jesus?' Did they know I was a Christian or were they assuming that most English people were? Was it genuine interest or the result of a made-up mind? In that instance I was literally saved by the bell. I was not very sure I wanted to continue the discussion with the individual who was firing the questions.

Celebrating success

The end of the year meant certificates and celebrations. This is how Hanan summed it all up:

> Reflecting on the past year . . . there have been many highs and lows, laughter and tears, happiness and frustrations. Working in Peckham with Muslim pupils has at the best of times been hard and exhausting work but at the same time watching some pupils mature while others change their attitude or become more confident, as well as seeing pupils develop their education, has been a memorable experience and a pleasure to watch.[8]

Everything was set for the prize-giving. I was wearing my Palestinian-embroidered kameez shirt and greeted everyone with *salaam aleikum* (peace be upon you). At the ceremony two of the teenage girls with some of the worst attitude stood up and sang 'The greatest love of all'. It was about dignity and self-respect. They had practised hard and put their heart and soul into it, and you could tell It was real. It brought a lump to my throat. Nemata, bless her, stood up and spoke kind words about me being a wonderful teacher and that I gave her confidence by the things I said.

And then it was over. Sadly, after a three-year project cycle (as often in voluntary organisations), the funding for the supplementary school had come to an end, but the experience for everyone had been an education in every sense. SMWA otherwise continues to go from strength to strength, Hanan is now married with a baby and working hard – and I'm qualified and still teaching ESOL in multi faith South London.

Response by Hanan Kasmi

'Mint tea or coke?'

'Coke, of course,' was my response to one of my cousins as we made our way to the roof terrace of a café in Tangier. Morocco, my country of origin, was a place I had visited numerous times, but it was my first time to this café and I was looking forward to taking in the beautiful views of this great city. Then I saw something that made me stop and stare. Was that a St George's flag blowing in the wind? I was quite confused, but it was definitely there atop an old Andalusian-style building that looked like the minaret of a mosque. Curiosity got the better of me as I left my cousins and set off to find the building.

I made my way through the busy, bustling streets of the old Madinah really excited at the prospect of seeing something English, as everything in Morocco is either in Arabic or French. When I got to the gates a plaque read: 'St Andrew's Church – English Church'. Wow, I thought, here hidden in the heart of Tangier is an old English church, and I wondered why I had not at least heard of it before. I felt quite exhilarated as I stood there, but it was closed so I made my way back to the café with the intention of returning very soon.

When I went back I learned that the great-grandfather of King Mohammed, Sultan Hassan I, had given the land to Queen Victoria during the 1880s to build a church. The country's top artisans and craftsmen were brought in from Fez to build this Anglo- and Andalusian-style building. As I sat inside it I thought it weird that, although I had been born and bred in South London where there are dozens of churches, old and new, the first one I would ever enter would be in Morocco. But I felt completely at home, totally comfortable, at peace and close to God: the same feelings as when I enter a mosque. It was in this church that I realised the essential oneness of humanity, and that you don't have to be Muslim to feel or experience the greatness of God.

While at SMWA I would sometimes think of my experience at St Andrew's Church, especially when Helen and I would finish talking about the day, the pupils, the parents, the curriculum, and so on. The discussion always seemed to lead on to bigger, more complex questions, and we both found solace in having God in our lives. I felt so close to Helen because I felt that she truly understood how important my faith is to me and how important it is to live by it and for it. At SMWA Helen was quite simply an integral part of our family who worked hard to enhance the lives of our children, and for that we were always grateful.

Growing up is hard enough, but growing up during these turbulent times and negotiating where you belong was something that many of the young people spoke to me about. Some said that their faith was more important than the country they lived in, whereas others argued that they were British first. I would challenge them to think more about this: does it have to be either/or? I would retell the story of the old English church in Muslim Morocco and we would talk about the many mosques here in London, and we would conclude that people who have different faiths, cultures and languages have always lived together. Thus the dilemma as to whether they are British or Muslim became quite spurious as these young people began to accept and see themselves as simply British and Muslim and proud to be South Londoners.

Further reading

Muslims in London, 2006, London: Greater London Authority.

SMWA newsletters, leaflets, documents, annual reports and website: www.smwa.org.uk.

Southwark Analytical Hub: www.southwark.gov.uk.

Sarah Thorley, 2007, *Improved Understanding of South London's Multi Faith Situation*, London: South London Inter Faith Group: available from South London Inter Faith Group, 24 Holmewood Gardens, London SW2 3RS.

Notes

1 *The Koran*, 1974, translated by N. J. Dawood, fourth revised edition, Harmondsworth: Penguin, p. 363.

2 www.smwa.org.uk.

3 SMWA Annual Report, 2003–2004.

4 Southwark Analytical Hub, General Population: www.southwark. gov.uk.

5 *Muslims in London*, 2006, London: Greater London Authority, p. 55.

6 SMWA education newsletter, December 2003.

7 *Muslims in London*, p. 47.

8 SMWA education newsletter, June 2004.

10 In Prison Together
Working towards an inclusive chaplaincy

ALISON TYLER

with a response by Ahtsham Ali

Just then a lawyer stood up to test Jesus. 'Teacher,' he said, 'What must I do to inherit eternal life?' He said to him, 'What is written in the law? What do you read there?' He answered, 'You shall love the Lord your God with all your heart, and with all your soul, and with all your strength, and with all your mind; and your neighbour as yourself.' And he said to him, 'You have given the right answer; do this, and you will live.'

Luke 10.25–28

We have ordained a law and assigned a path for each of you. Had Allah pleased, He could have made you one nation: but it is His wish to prove you by that which He has bestowed upon you. Vie with each other in good works, for to Allah you shall all return and He will declare to you what you have disagreed about.

The Holy Qur'an, Sura 5.48[1]

In the weeks leading up to Christmas a couple of years ago I realised that on Christmas Eve and Christmas Day there was no one at the prison to assist me with making the worship festive and special. I was providing temporary cover for Brixton Prison, which did not at the time have an Anglican Chaplain in post. On Christmas Eve there would be just me and an organist, joined on Christmas Day by the bishop. I shared this problem with Robin, our Hindu volunteer who visits prisoners at weekends, providing pastoral care and moral support. 'Leave it with me,' he said and I stopped worrying.

On Christmas Eve and again on Christmas Day, Robin and a group of friends came and sang carols with the prisoners. It was a great success and the prisoners were greatly appreciative.

Robin has very inclusive views. When I first met him he was running a multi faith group for prisoners who talked, each from his own faith perspective, of their journey to faith. They shared their stories and discovered they had much in common. He has been working voluntarily for over ten years offering unconditional support and concern to prisoners of all faiths and none. Robin works on the basis that all religious experience is significant and should be encouraged, and that there is much practice in common between the faiths, despite doctrinal and theological differences.

The changing face of prison chaplaincy

It is only relatively recently that this kind of activity has been possible. Under the 1952 Prison Act a prison chaplain would have been a male Anglican, paid a salary by the Prison Service. Other chaplains from different Christian traditions could have been appointed additionally according to local need, again paid a salary by the Prison Service. Any other faith contribution would have been made either by an unpaid volunteer or by a fee-paid visiting minister. Gradually the provision of chaplaincy services has become more open and more reflective of the changing nature of our communities and prison populations, with the appointment, first, of other salaried Christian (Roman Catholic and Free Church) chaplains, and finally salaried chaplains from other faiths.

There are now more than 30 full-time Muslim chaplains and a large number of part-timers, reflecting the fact that approximately 10 per cent of prisoners are Muslims. There are now full-time and part-time Hindu and Sikh chaplains. The Buddhist community provides chaplains via the Angulimala Association. Chaplains from smaller faith communities are also appointed according to local need. Despite the very few Quakers or Salvationists among prisoners, both traditions have a very long history of working within prisons, with those of any faith or none. For a long time the Prison Service has had excellent policies on diversity, but it is only recently that these policies are being put into practice and prison chaplaincy work has become pioneering in the multi faith aspects of working in the public services. More money is spent in the UK on prison chaplaincy services than in any other comparable system.

The present Chaplain General to the Prison Service, the Venerable William Noblett, was appointed with a specific remit to develop multi faith chaplaincy provision. Soon afterwards he produced a short document entitled 'Principles for an Inclusive Chaplaincy as suggested by the Chaplain General' (see Appendix, page 118) which has become the basis for current practice. This outlines the need for chaplains to cater for the faith needs of the changing prison population. He also expanded the Chaplaincy Council, a consultation body, including leaders of the main faiths, which advises the Prison Service on policy concerning chaplaincy and faith-related issues. The faith leaders represented on the Council endorse those who represent their faiths as prison chaplains. None of us can work as chaplains in prison without the endorsement of our faith community.

Inevitably, given the historical context of prison chaplaincy, there remain tough residual issues. In the main these are related to the perception among some that the Anglican chaplains are advantaged by virtue of their long-standing organisation and the continuing, though declining, position of the Church of England as the Established Church. The perception of an imbalance of power within a chaplaincy team remains one of the factors most likely to cause disputes. Anglicans would possibly now challenge the notion of being advantaged as there are principles in place to ensure, as far as possible, a balanced and proportionate allocation of chaplaincy time and resources among the different faith communities. Given the resource difficulties of the Prison Service caused by the relentless pressure of numbers, there will continue to be robust discussions and competition in this area.

It is, however, no longer the case that the Anglican chaplain is automatically the Co-ordinating or Lead Chaplain as the criteria are based not on faith but on competence and the role is determined at the discretion of the Governor of each establishment. Job advertisements no longer specify that the Anglican chaplain's post will automatically be combined with that of Coordinating Chaplain. There are now several Roman Catholic and Muslim Coordinating Chaplains and their numbers are set to increase as more of them gain the necessary experience and team competencies.

The climate has changed completely since the 1950s. As chaplains we all now have the duty and responsibility to accept the faith of others, to be seen to do so, and actively to ensure that all are able to worship freely and in a dignified and decent fashion.

When I first started as a chaplain at Brixton Prison in 1999 the only full-time chaplains were Christian. Three years later the first full-time Muslim chaplain had been appointed. One of my first team assessments at Wormwood Scrubs in 2002 highlighted the need for a full-time Muslim chaplain as a matter of urgency. He was appointed within twelve months. Between 2002 and 2006 the Muslim population at Wormwood Scrubs rose from around 100 to around 250. There was a similar rate of growth in Sikh and Hindu prisoners, and increasing the chaplaincy provision for them became a similar priority. There has been a full-time Hindu chaplain for London for about two years, and in July 2007 the first full-time Sikh chaplain for London started work.

Volunteer support

The presence of full-time chaplains of any faith in a prison does two things, both important. First, the religious needs of the prisoners are given proper consideration and can be better dealt with. Second, the faith community outside can be mobilised to become involved in the prison as volunteers, and outside the prison as part of the process of welcoming, supporting and resettling those who are released back into the community from which they came.

The issue of resettlement has become more significant on the Prison Service agenda over the past few years. It is no longer thought sufficient to keep people securely in custody and then release them without making any provision for their resettlement. Government policy and thinking has increasingly seen resettlement as the responsibility of the whole community, involving not just statutory agencies (Probation, local authorities and social services) but a whole range of voluntary and faith-based organisations as well. Prison chaplaincies have responded, along with community-based faith groups, by seeking to set up community chaplaincies (officially defined as independent faith-based charitable voluntary organisations) to help with re-settlement in a variety of ways, from befriending to intensive mentoring. The services their volunteers provide range from the very simple – support and companionship as the ex-offender seeks to access the resources needed in terms of finding accommodation, a job, education and training – to the more complex, involving needs assessments and specialist referrals. There are several very good examples of the work of community chaplaincy, notably the Swansea, North Staffordshire and West Yorkshire projects, which enable individuals to find accommodation and work and create pre-release relationships with prisoners which carry on outside the prison. There are many similar projects throughout the country.

The new National Offender Management Service will be seeking to engage with and even commission some faith-based community chaplaincies in this work. In order to attract public support and funding, these projects will need to be multi faith, serving the needs of those of all faiths and none, while at the same time recognising and meeting the needs of particular faith groups. The volunteers need to be recruited and trained accordingly, to work both inside and outside the prison.

Good volunteers are difficult to recruit and hard to train as everyone has an individual view of prison. Some may think they are above the rules because, after all, they are people of faith. However, we *all* have to carry our keys attached to our belts (not loose in our pockets), keep our home contact details and those of our colleagues confidential, and avoid being recruited by prisoners to help them bend the rules. To be fair, most volunteers do all of these things, and more, without difficulty, and they work unfailingly hard. It is the near-disasters that are unfortunately most memorable, and have become one of my preoccupations as a training officer. Take the example of the delightful woman who said she had let a prisoner use her mobile phone, as he had had his taken off him! The rule is that you leave your phone at the prison gate and under no circumstances do you make a call for a prisoner, or let him/her make an unsupervised call of any kind.

There are constraints to working in prison and we have to abide by them. In the preamble to one of my training courses I begin by reminding the participants that a prison is a formal public setting and rules need to be kept for the sake of all involved. It is not like going to the pub to meet a mate, and never can be, no matter how comfortable you become in the prison or how concerned you are to affirm and accept the prisoner you are working with. It will always be work, and will always need to be performed within prescribed boundaries.

Challenging issues

The prison population is a microcosm of the pluralistic and diverse community from which the prisoners come. This micro-cosm of people of all faiths and none is compelled to live closely together within the prison walls, but there are surprisingly few situations of tension and conflict.

When things do go wrong it is often in unexpected ways, for example by the erroneous conflation of race/ethnicity and reli-gion. You cannot assume that no Muslim prisoners will be white: 12 per cent of the Muslim population in the UK is white. In this instance to challenge a white prisoner who registers as Muslim can cause difficulties, as can the assumption that all South Asian prisoners are Muslim: they may not be. Indeed, they could be Hindu, Sikh, Christian, Buddhist, or of another faith; or they might have no religious affiliation. To make assumptions with-out checking causes justifiable irritation about stereotyping. There is also potential for misunderstanding about the apparent 'religious' convictions of some young people who name their gangs as if they had a genuine religious affiliation.

Recently the sharing of 'sacred space' in a cramped prison environment has been a challenging issue. The different views among faith groups about statues, candles, pictures and images, and how they should be regarded and treated, has caused ten-sions among some groups of prisoners who, due to the rapid spread of rumours, are swift to assume disrespect when perhaps it was only lack of information that caused the problem. One of the teaching roles of chaplaincies is to educate both staff and prisoners about different faith communities. In my case this fre-quently involves trying to help people understand that 'things' only have religious or other significance if we ascribe it to them: of themselves they are merely attractive arrangements of colour or shape, but they need to be treated with respect because of the significance that they may have for someone else.

If, for Christians generally, the challenge of the twentieth century was learning ecumenical dialogue, then the greater, more complex and urgent task of the twenty-first century will be learning the skills of inter faith dialogue. Within the close confines of the diverse imprisoned community this is increasing-ly both essential and possible, and a prison is thus a very good place in which to be attempting the dialogue.

At a meeting of the London Area Chaplains, a quarterly event when all the chaplains of all the faiths from London prisons come together to discuss issues of common concern, an ordinand from the Church of Ireland, in his first week of placement in prison ministry in England, was visiting us. He commented spontaneously on the respect and concern the chaplains had shown, not only for one another but also for the interests of those of another faith who were not represented, and said that it had not been what he had expected. He was very impressed by the naturalness of the proceedings. There was no sense in which he felt the shared concern was forced or imposed. The next edition of the Chaplaincy Newsletter contained some ten main items, five of which related to multi faith issues.

Working in a multi faith context is now, for those of us in public service, a well-established fact of life. It is enshrined in the Prison Service rules, and reinforced by various formal orders. It is supported through the diversity policies to which we are held accountable through the internal audit system and via the Chief Inspector of Prisons, whose reports feature the extent to which our practice reflects the policy.

That is the formal framework for the work. We then have to translate it into practice, which is where it can become difficult. In 'outside' situations, such as in parishes, you can more often than not choose whether you want to engage with those of other faiths. In the prison context there is no choice. As with our relatives, so with our work colleagues, we have to work with whomever we are given. This is one of the reasons why it is difficult to predict success. We can try hard to apply all the best practices in which we have been trained, but successful teams are dependent on the relationships between their members. We may strongly advocate working with those of different faiths, and we may really want to do it, but personal chemistry and temperamental differences between team members may still make the work difficult, despite real effort.

Often the areas of difficulty are not really about faith differences at all but about cultural, gender or similar issues. It takes real energy and attentive listening to understand the issues of individuals who are culturally very distant from each other. One of the other frequently overlooked problems is that faith leaders are inexperienced at being managed employees. As faith leaders we are too used to being the boss in our respective communities. The result is that we are unwilling to allow ourselves to be managed or to accept that we are employed by, paid by and accountable to the Prison Service to provide a service. We are therefore judged, not on our faith, but on the professional performance of our duties. We are required, for example, to lead worship, to teach or to preach, and it is sad but true that, for the prison, the important thing is merely that the activity takes place. No one other than our faith leaders is much concerned about the content, unless it advocates riots or foments other forms of discontent.

Working collaboratively

Those of us who come to prison ministry from the Christian tradition do so because we believe that we are called by God to this work: called to witness, through the power of the Holy Spirit, to the ultimate significance of Jesus Christ as the incarnate word and wisdom of God. It is this faith that informs and motivates our ministry: we are to be Christ for our community, in this case our prison. Because our faith is incarnational, our practice is relational. Through Christ we are called into new relationships with God and with one another. Genuine relationships are rooted in openness, honesty and mutuality, and all our different faith traditions have in common a regard for relationships characterised by compassion and generosity of spirit.

The ethical dimensions of faith as lived by those of all traditions are a good basis for beginning the inter faith dialogue that we need to have. Many theologians have also observed the commonality of the mystical experience among people of faith. Those of all faiths who take God seriously are aware that *now* our knowledge is partial,[2] and those of us who are honest freely admit that this is our experience too. We come to the conversation as those who seek the truth, who seek to know God, and our different faith traditions have this search in common although we may well be making apparently different journeys.

Given the location of our work it is impossible not to be aware of the current issues around terrorism and extremist prisoners, especially considering the way in which such issues are written up in the popular press and the reactions that this engenders. Those prisoners who are seen as Al Qaeda-inspired terrorists, or similar violent extremists, generate particular problems for the Prison Service as it has to combine being fair with being vigilant and ensuring the safety of others. Prisons are also likely places for the exploitation of the vulnerable and disadvantaged, and again vigilance and fairness have to be exercised.

Relatively few of us have direct experience of working with extremist or very dangerous prisoners, but we are all part of a wider movement within prison chaplaincy to model alternative ways of working: actually to be doing collaboratively all that we can, while at the same time respecting the integrity of each faith tradition and celebrating their diversity. As people of faith we are those who have the responsibility to demonstrate other ways of being that do not involve discrimination, injustice, exploitation and violence. Working effectively as a multi faith team can be both an example and a model for others, and a gift from all of our faith communities to the places in which we operate.

As there is much potential for friction between the different groups of prisoners it is particularly important that we as chaplains are seen to work collaboratively, especially during times of wider social unease. There have been times when issues have arisen when one faith group has felt insulted by members of another, even over something relatively trivial; and there have been confrontations between prisoners on their landings which need to be handled very sensitively. Rumours spread very quickly in small overcrowded communities. At such times it needs to be more apparent than usual that we, as chaplains, hold one another in trust and mutual respect. One of the ways in which we can demonstrate this is by routinely sharing the work. When I was working at Wormwood Scrubs we took turns on a rota basis at visiting the new arrivals, regardless of their faith tradition. This involved welcoming them and dealing with any immediate issues if we could, and offering to send them their own faith chaplain only if they asked for or needed him or her for a particular reason. We wanted them to know, from the beginning, that any one of us would be able and happy to offer support to anyone who asked for it.

There is little time in a chaplaincy team for theological reflection. The pressure of numbers, the constraints of the prison core day (the time in the day when all the basic tasks of care, self-maintenance and learning have to be done, when the prisoners are unlocked and the staffing levels are at their highest), the many different combinations of working hours of chaplains and their availability, all conspire against considered discussion or even thought. It was not until I sat down to write this chapter that I was able to put my many disconnected thoughts and reflections into any kind of order. I realised, though, quite early in my prison ministry, that it is by working together that we develop our inter faith relationships. The urgency of the shared task focuses the mind and encapsulates some of the possibilities of learning *from* those of other faith traditions, rather than merely learning *about* them.

This becomes increasingly possible as more chaplains from different faith communities are appointed. It was very apparent once we had a full-time Hindu chaplain working in the London Area that he brought a completely different dimension to the work. The Hindu tradition is, in many respects, extremely inclusive, and is therefore very open to working together and sharing the tasks. It is especially encouraging to experience joint Hindu and Sikh celebrations of common festivals and common cultural events. It was good for the team and for the prisoners to share these experiences.

Actually doing the work is fascinating, rewarding, frustrating and fun, and it depends for its success largely on the quality of the relationships between the team members and the attitudes they bring to the work. I really enjoyed the challenge of managing a collection of people from different faith backgrounds so that they experienced it both as fair and as operating in their interests. If I didn't manage it properly they were swift to complain to my line manager and I had to put it right. The frustration lay in not succeeding, even though you had tried your best. It is a challenge, but fun, to find a restaurant for a shared meal that can cope with all our dietary requirements – including kosher, halal, organic gluten-free and vegetarian, to name but four – so that we could have a meal out together. Bring and share was easier, although it had health and safety obligations attached to it. Doing the work together over a period of time makes it increasingly successful. Success breeds confidence and trust and incrementally the relationships develop and expand. We do not have to believe in the same things as our colleagues, but we do have to believe that their faith is as important to them as ours is to us.

It is not possible to legislate for open minds and positive attitudes (would that it were), but I have always tried to encourage and affirm them wherever I have found them in the teams I have worked with. This does not mean watering down our own faith or skimping on our own religious practice in order somehow to make those of other faiths 'feel more comfortable'. That is not how it works. In order to make our faith make sense to others we

need to be as good at it as we can be and to practise it properly
and fully. In this way we show each other the very best that our
tradition has to offer and enable each other to get a real sense of
why we believe and practise our particular faith.

Keeping up the momentum

The principles for good multi faith practice are now established
in prison chaplaincy, and it is truly amazing how far we have
managed to come in a relatively short time. As someone who has
been part of the process thus far, I have really enjoyed it and feel
very privileged to have been involved in such an interesting and
challenging experience. It gets better as it continues, even though
progress is gradual and there are setbacks. Continuing training
and support for teams, and increasing numbers of non-Angli-
cans taking their part as Co-ordinating Chaplains with experienced colleagues providing mentoring and support, are needed
to keep up the momentum and move the work further forward. I
hope to be a part of it for several more years to come. Where else
could I find, without difficulty, such a great collection of diverse
and interesting people with whom to discuss so many different
things, including religion, and with whom to explore new ways
of working and of deepening understanding?

Since taking on the role of Learning and Development Officer
for prison chaplains I have found increasingly interesting the
number of common practices within faith communities and the
priorities that they have in common. In a recent World Faiths
course it was clear that prayer, study of scripture, communal
worship and upright moral living are the foundations of most
faith communities, and were important for all of the participants.
The best moment for me was the expressions on the faces of some
of my more evangelical colleagues (of several different faiths)
when told by the visiting rabbi how difficult it is, and deliberately so, to convert to Judaism. Both he and a Muslim colleague
recounted stories of individuals who had converted in order to
marry either a Jew or a Muslim and had been disappointed by
how badly their intended spouses practised the faiths that they
were trying so hard to learn. It made me realise the responsibility
we have not only to be faithful but also to be seen to be.

Response by Ahtsham Ali, Muslim Advisor to the Prison Service

The Revd Alison Tyler has encapsulated in a relatively short piece the most pertinent issues, the pleasures and the challenges of working in a multi faith chaplaincy within prisons. She has provided an excellent historical overview of how multi faith chaplaincy emerged from an essentially Anglican prison chaplaincy.

This exciting and pioneering area of work is deeply undervalued at a time when the need for it is so crucial. Britain, Europe and the world have never been so culturally mixed as they are now. We have never had access to so many different cultures, races and faiths. And yet most countries of the world do not embrace the different faiths that their citizens may possess. Alison mentions how 'very impressed' the ordinand from the Church of Ireland was when he witnessed first-hand a multi faith London Area Chaplaincy meeting. This does not surprise me. Despite our sense of our own shortcomings we are in fact world leaders in developing multi faith chaplaincy to the extent that we have. A trip to any international conference on prison chaplaincy shows how poorly developed most countries are in this field.

The Prison Service is the largest employer of chaplains in the UK. It is, no doubt, a different world, and Alison hits the nail on the head when she says that, within the prison, 'as with our relatives, so with our colleagues, you have to work with whomever you are given'. Prison multi faith chaplaincy will most definitely go beyond the cups of tea and polite chitchat that often accompany many inter faith dialogue meetings. In the latter you interact for a bit, for an afternoon, maybe for a few days, and then you go home to your flock and your comfort zone. However, in prison, day in, day out, you have to work cheek by jowl 'with whomever you are given' and there is no escape from it. And therein lies the difference. This daily interaction with colleagues from all the different world faiths, in an environment that is often manic and tense, 'reaches parts other multi faith work cannot reach'.

Alison talks about the inexperience of faith leaders at being managed employees. Certainly that is there, but for Muslim prison chaplaincy there are also other relative inexperiences. Although historically, going back almost a thousand years, we as Muslims had a rich heritage of inter faith dialogue, this cannot be said of the past few hundred years. Hence even in the case of intra faith dialogue (between denominations), let alone inter faith dialogue, we are the 'new kids on the block'. There are also differences in key concepts, and it is important that in the evolution of prison chaplaincy non-Christian faiths are not trapped within Christian models and frameworks. As Muslim chaplains, for example, we have no concept of a 'calling'. Our theologies and laws of interaction with non-Muslim communities were shaped at the height of Muslim civilisation and political supremacy. Hence it is difficult to translate to current circumstances without amendments.

But what is the essential component in multi faith working? It is, as Alison describes, that chaplains have to 'believe that their faith is as important to them as ours is to us'. This is the most important concept for people to grasp and the most difficult to practise: to try to understand others, to grasp why it is that they believe this and that. In the words of Atticus Finch, the hero of Harper Lee's novel *To Kill a Mockingbird*, 'you never really understood a person until you climbed into his skin and walked around in it'.

One cannot overestimate the importance of this interaction between different faiths within prison chaplaincy as it evolves and progresses. It teaches us how to deal with differences; how to be neighbours; and above all it allows us to be comfortable with the fact that we are not all clones. It will shape the future of who we are, as people, and as a nation. As the wise Chinese saying goes: 'One generation plants the trees, and the next generation benefits from the shade.'

Appendix

Principles for an Inclusive Chaplaincy as suggested by the Chaplain General:

- recognition and celebration of diversity
- respect for the integrity of each tradition
- the value of each member is affirmed
- there is giving and accepting of responsibility
- empowerment, through the recognition of each chaplain's ministry, is implicit
- the skills, gifts, talents, competencies of team members are enabled and used appropriately

- decision making, whenever possible, is that of the Team and done in a collegial way
- the allocation, and re-allocation of budget resources is 'transparent' and a Team responsibility
- Team members believe chaplaincy must show an alternative way of working within the institution, and serve as a positive example to staff and prisoners
- people, not power, lies at the heart of the chaplaincy
- collaborative working is seen as the norm
- accountability is mutual
- communication is open and honest
- the principles and practice of RESPOND, RESPECT, and the Inter Faith Network Guidelines, are integral to all that is done.

Further reading

Hans Küng, 1993, *Christianity and the World Religions*, London: SCM Press.
Eleanor Nesbitt, 2003, *Interfaith Pilgrims*, London: Quaker Books.
Jonathan Sacks, 2002, *The Dignity of Difference*, London: Continuum.
www.hmprisonservice.gov.uk (for prison information and statistics).
www.interreligiousinsight.org.

Notes

1 *The Koran*, 1974, translated by N. J. Dawood, fourth revised edition, Harmondsworth: Penguin, p. 393.
2 1 Corinthians 13.12.

11 Neighbours and Friends Together

The London Peace Pagoda and All Saints' Church, Battersea

ALAN GADD

with a response by Bhikkhu G. Nagase

Not everyone who says to me, 'Lord, Lord', will enter the kingdom of heaven, but only one who does the will of my Father in heaven.

Matthew 7.21

All beings can expiate misdeeds, perform good, and attain Buddhahood by the merits of this Sutra. It does not matter whether they are wise or not or whether they believe the Sutra or reject it.

A verse for opening the Lotus Sutra[1]

It is just before seven o'clock on a Saturday morning in June as I park my car and walk along beside the River Thames in Battersea Park to reach the Peace Pagoda. As always, the Pagoda looks stunningly beautiful. It has an elegant, double-roof structure and a pinnacle that rises more than 30 metres above the ground. The top of the pinnacle and the wind-bells at the octagonal roof corners are gilded, as of course are the large statues of the Buddha in the four niches. The four statues depict the Buddha's birth, his first sermon, his enlightenment and his passing away.

When I arrive, I find two people already there, one of whom I discover to be a monk of the Nipponzan Myohoji order. He had arrived in London two days before from Sicily. I offer help, and he sets me to work taping together the two halves of long branches of pink flowering cherry, the paper petals having been made into flowers before being brought to the scene. Later four double-ended branches would be wired into position across each of six beautifully painted boxes, and the boxes would be lifted on poles and placed at intervals along the front of the pagoda, quickly creating a joyous setting. Just before I arrived, the work had been moved under the shelter of one of the Park's fine plane trees at the onset of one of the heavy showers of rain that were to be a feature of much of the day.

The occasion is to be the twenty-second anniversary celebration of the London Peace Pagoda, and the ceremony is due to begin at two o'clock. The Pagoda is one of nearly a hundred all around the world built by monks, nuns and followers of Nipponzan Myohoji. The other Peace Pagoda in Britain is in Milton Keynes. The order was founded in the early part of the twentieth century within the Nichiren strand of Buddhism in Japan. The Founder and Preceptor was the Most Venerable Nichidatsu Fujii, often known by the name given to him by Mahatma Gandhi – 'Fujii Guruji'. Like their Founder, the monks and nuns are dedicated campaigners for peace; walking and demonstrating for peace issues around the world, and sometimes ending up in prison.

Within a further ten minutes two vehicles arrive on the scene. One is the blue minibus from All Saints' Church, Battersea Park, driven by Phillipe Cotgreave de Rahman, one of the All Saints' churchwardens, who is returning after having first arrived in the park at half past five that morning. Inside the minibus are part of the workforce Phillipe has gathered from among the All Saints' church members. Zam Hao, Naveed Solomondass and Merit Nwajohn dismount to help with the physical work, while Corinne Voilquin and Adelaide Davidson stay in the minibus and continue to the nearby small Dojo (temple) where they will prepare breakfast and assist with a variety of tasks. Stephen Hodnell, another friend of Phillipe, arrives separately to complete the early morning effort. The All Saints' contingent includes people with roots in Bangladesh, England, France, Ghana, Ireland, Myanmar, Nigeria and Pakistan, and I marvel again at the way God has brought people together from all corners of his world to make up today's church congregations in London. Talking to Phillipe, I learn that the flowers have been made during the previous week by a group that includes, from All Saints', Cynthia Fernandes, Amy Lewis, Neng Pi and several children, thus adding India and Jamaica to the rich variety of cultural origins.

The other vehicle to arrive is a white hired van, driven by Bhikkhu Nagase, resident monk in Battersea Park for the whole twenty-two years since it was founded, living at the Dojo and looking after the Pagoda. ('Bhikkhu' is the title for a Buddhist monk.) 'Looking after the Pagoda', by the way, is no mean task. There are frequent episodes of desecration, with graffiti or worse, to add anxiety and difficult extra work to the routine cleaning that any outdoor monument requires. For Bhikkhu Nagase the task is made even harder by his incomprehension of the cultural situation, so different from that in Japan where vandalism of a holy place is unthinkable. He has often wished that the park's security cameras could be better placed for the protection of the Pagoda.

The white van is packed with chairs, and will return again several times during the next hour or so with more chairs, tables, decorations, devotional equipment and an outdoor PA system.

I leave the scene just in time to avoid the car parking charges that begin at nine o'clock and spend the morning attending to other tasks. Just as I am leaving I meet Conal Percy, Suzanne Keys and Finbar (aged two) arriving on their bicycles. This family are well known to worshippers at Southwark Anglican Cathedral but keep a close link also with All Saints', Battersea. Their timing is perfect as they can keep a watch on the developing ceremonial arena while the rest of the early gang go off to the Dojo to partake of Adelaide's and Corinne's breakfast.

When I return by bus in the early afternoon the anniversary ceremony has just started. I know from previous years that it will fall into three sections. For the first hour the Nipponzan Myohoji monks will lead us in chanting from the Lotus Sutra, in offerings of flowers, incense and perfumes, and in walking around the Peace Pagoda while chanting 'Namu Myo Ho Ren Ge Kyo', which is the sacred title of the Lotus Sutra. Other Buddhist monks, from Tibetan, Sri Lankan, Thai and Vietnamese traditions, wearing a range of orange, saffron and deep red robes, will also offer chanting. An address will be given in Japanese by the Venerable Gyosei Masunaga Shonin, the elder monk of the order, followed by an English translation by Shigeo Kobayashi, the unflappable master of ceremonies with many years of experience of these occasions. All this unfolds as expected. One of the familiar faces among the Nipponzan Myohoji monks is Bhikkhu

Seiji Handa who, sadly, will die only two months later in a tragic accident, trapped under a tractor while mowing the grass next to the Peace Pagoda in Milton Keynes.

As the second section starts, headed 'Inter Faith Prayers for World Peace', I become more alert because Phillipe and I are going to make a contribution. The programme says that a prayer for peace will be offered by the Revd Anand and the Revd Jessie, the newly arrived priests at All Saints', but sadly the Revd Anand suffered an injury to his foot a few days previously. This is to be one of three Christian prayers (Anglican, Roman Catholic and Quaker) along with prayers from Baha'i, Brahma Kumari, Hindu, Muslim, Jain and Sikh traditions. When our turn comes, I introduce our contribution and Phillipe prays a 'Set All Free' prayer that marks the two hundredth anniversary of the Act of Parliament to abolish the slave trade. We felt that peace can only be established for the future if there is an honest facing up to the history of what has been done in the past and still affects the present.

The inter faith prayers for peace are followed by a number of speeches. Then, the final section of the ceremony consists of a cultural programme of recitation, music and dance. Again I am keyed up because I know that two contributions have been prepared that involve young people from All Saints'. Melba and Mayola Fernandes, and Alice Green and her friend Amelia recite 'Be Alive!' in the forthright style pioneered with young people at All Saints' by Canon Ivor Smith-Cameron. Later Melba and Mayola appear again, with Natasha and Casmira Ivan, all in colourful Rajastan costumes in a dance set to 'If I were a butterfly', introduced by Chitra Ivan and choreographed by Chella Pichamuthu.

After tea and refreshments I am happily making my way back to the 137 bus when I spot Conal and Suzanne and Finbar also making ready to depart. I realise that they have not left the park all day, and I discover later that neither has Corinne. I am touched by the commitment of the church members to support Bhikkhu Nagase in every aspect of the event, and I feel really grateful to Phillipe who had drawn us all together in this involvement. As the company disperses, gifts of fruit and packets of tea, which had formed part of the ceremonial offering, are distributed in a free and generous manner. Flowers are taken to All Saints' Church where they beautify the Sunday Eucharist the next morning and draw more members of the church into the experience.

On the bus I am in pensive mood. So this had been the twenty-second anniversary of the London Peace Pagoda, built in Battersea Park in 1985. At that time the Park had been run by the Greater London Council (GLC), but soon afterwards the GLC was abolished and the park came under the control of Wandsworth Council. The last deputy leader of the GLC, Illtyd Harrington, played an important role in the establishment of the Pagoda, and has remained committed to this Buddhist presence ever since. He had made a short speech during the afternoon, as had Bruce Kent, of the Movement for the Abolition of War. Another, very encouraging, speech had been given by Councillor Stuart Thom, the current Mayor of Wandsworth. He conveyed a sense of pride at the Pagoda's presence in Wandsworth and a sense of commitment to its support. This will be really good news if it is carried through, because it has not always been the case.

I think about Bhikkhu Nagase; about his commitment to peace and to inter faith engagement, about his dedicated support of the South London Inter Faith Group, and about his participation worldwide in long 'marches for peace'. I think of the many individual friends of his, of many different cultures and faiths, who enjoy calling in at the Dojo, where he welcomes them with a prayer, a sweet, and a chat. What a remarkable man he is.

My thoughts move on to reflect on All Saints' Church. All Saints' is an Anglican church located just outside Battersea Park. Working with Ivor Smith-Cameron, I had been a priest there from 1990 until 2005. From 2002 All Saints' had been richly blessed by the extended placement of the Revd Premraj and the Revd Deborah, with their family, from Chennai, South India. Prem and Deborah continued to lead All Saints' until 2006. Then, after a gap of nine months, the Revd Anand and the Revd Jessie had arrived from Leicester at the beginning of February. Over the years a wealth of lay leadership has been nurtured by encouraging 'participation' as a guiding principle, with the formal training courses offered by the diocese a much-valued resource.

All Saints' Church has developed a positive stance towards inter faith relationships. Guests from other faiths have been routinely invited to major occasions in the life of the church, and other faiths have often been remembered in prayer at the Sunday Eucharist. Against this background, there is no surprise that there has been a growing friendship with Bikkhu Nagase. The friendship has centred on a sharing in each other's religious ceremonies, but it also includes participating together in meetings and demonstrations.

Over the years, members of All Saints' have taken part in ceremonies at the Peace Pagoda and the Dojo, including those on New Year's Day, the Founder's commemoration on 9 January, the bean throwing ceremony, and Buddha's birthday. The anniversary ceremony, on a Saturday in June, has always been a great highlight of the year, but the other, deeply moving occasion is on Nagasaki Day, 9 August. In commemoration of those who died from the second of the atomic bombs dropped on Japan in 1945, and those who suffered terribly from the radiation afterwards, there is a procession from Westminster Cathedral and then a ceremony at the Pagoda. This ceremony leads on to the release of floating lanterns on the River Thames. By this stage darkness has fallen and, depending on the wind and the tide, the result is spectacularly beautiful. A lantern is released for the year 1945 and for each year since – one extra lantern each year.

As part of the other side of the relationship, Bhikkhu Nagase has been an active participant in services and events at All Saints' Church, including Sunday Eucharists, the Easter Dawn Liturgy, Christmas Day lunch, ecumenical events in the Battersea Riverside Churches Together programme, jubilees, farewells, and welcomes. As part of the worship he chants 'Namu Myo Ho Ren Ge Kyo', accompanied by drumming and bells.

An issue arose in connection with a Confirmation service at All Saints'. Clergy and confirmands from three neighbouring churches were present. Nagase attended and I invited him to chant towards the end of the service. The presiding bishop took it completely in his stride, and adopted a very gracious manner towards Nagase; but I received a complaint afterwards from one of the clergy, ostensibly on behalf of some of his congregation. I agreed that in future I would consult about any content from other faiths in joint services. There was no change in practice for All Saints' own worship week by week. This episode was illustrative, of course, of the fact that there are both positive and negative responses among Christians to people of other faiths taking part in Christian worship, or to the use of a suitable prayer or reading from another faith as an ingredient in Christian worship.

During 2002 there was a major redevelopment of the northern half of Battersea Park, leading to the Peace Pagoda being inaccessible to the public. I was delighted when Bhikkhu Nagase asked

if the Pagoda's anniversary ceremony that year could be celebrated in All Saints' Church. It seemed to be a wonderful expression of All Saints' and the Peace Pagoda being 'neighbours and
friends together'.

The ceremony went ahead very successfully in the church. Of
course, the particular character of the church was very helpful in
this. It was built in the 1970s as a 50ft square shell, with no
fixtures, plus some ancillary rooms. It replaced the original
church which had been damaged by fire in 1969. The 1970s
church was built alongside the 1890s vicarage and incorporated
what was originally the vicarage kitchen into the new church as
a 'second room', more recently known as the children's room.
Between 1990 and 2006 the remaining ground floor rooms of the
vicarage were also made available for communal use, so that the
house and the church became in effect a single unit of ministry
and mission.

Although the original concept of the 1970s worship space was
for a basically conventional layout, with rows of seating and an
altar at the front, the space has proved highly adaptable to other
approaches. It has been transformed into what in many ways is
now an ideal space within which multicultural worship (which
might include a variety of music and dance) may take place.
Having a space is one thing. Creating a climate for worship within that space is another very important matter. I would not say
that the climate is created and then we can worship: rather, the
climate evolves with the worship. If you were to enter the church
on a Sunday morning you would find the seating arranged in the
round, and many believe that this has been a crucial factor in the
distinctiveness of the worship at All Saints'.

Certain practicalities are essential. The space needs to be warm
and welcoming. The heating system must be kept effective so
that in winter worshippers can take off their overcoats and relax.
The carpet on the floor adds to the sense of warmth, but also has
a key role in muffling the sound of noisy shoes or of chairs being
moved. Lighting can make all the difference. Fabrics and objects
from around the world, with their beauty of colour, pattern and
shape, help greatly in the creation of the climate. When someone
from a particular part of the world enters the church and looks
around, the sight of something familiar gives a message of
welcome and belonging that words could never match.

All Saints' has benefited greatly from the work of a number of
artists. The seasonal hangings by Joyce Meadows and Unity

Spencer, the *Stations of the Cross* by Peter Wright, *Crucifixion in a Cornfield* and other works by Adam Boulter, and work by Nicola Clark, Jeremy Woodcock and others have made important contributions to the ambience. Michael Warren's painting of All Saints' in relationship to life in Battersea Park, which decorates the outside of the church at the front, expresses something of that atmosphere of welcome to those who approach and those who pass by. In 2002, Margaret Brodie co-ordinated 13 artists who are members or friends of All Saints' to contribute to a set of *Stations of the Resurrection*, designed to be hung in the church each year during the Great 50 Days, from Easter to Pentecost. None of the hangings or paintings inside the church is permanently placed. There is a rotation by season and theme, and this assists the images to be seen with fresh eyes on their reappearance. This procedure also makes space for the display of paintings that have sometimes been produced by young people at the weekly after-school session. The seven *Advent Antiphons* and four *Epiphany Themes* have been among the works of the junior artists of All Saints'.

Since there is just one space, all aspects of the church programme become interwoven. The worship space is also the place where hospitality is offered and food is shared. The same space serves as church, dining hall, dance floor, concert hall, lecture theatre and fairground, as the occasion requires. Then, as well as the church programme, the space is used in many other ways during the week: for yoga classes, taiji classes, residents' meetings, police and community meetings, Saturday workshops, children's groups, fund-raising concerts, and so on. These events draw upon the spirituality of the place. In many cases they also contribute positively to its climate.

This, then, was the space in which the Pagoda's 2002 anniversary ceremony took place. The programme was much as outlined above for 2007. Bhikkhu Nagase arranged for as much as possible of the usual decorations and offerings to be brought into the church and set up for the occasion. It was very beautifully done. With the obvious exception of the ceremonial walking around the Peace Pagoda, every other part of the traditional ceremony was fairly easy to adapt to the All Saints' setting. The cultural programme included beautiful dancing by devotees of the Thai Buddhist Temple in Wimbledon. The church was packed, with members of All Saints' congregation, friends of the Pagoda, and other visitors.

The following year things were back to normal, the restoration work in the park having been completed. Although there had been anxieties about the effects of the redevelopment on the Peace Pagoda, things turned out quite well. The new landscaping seemed sympathetic to the Pagoda's presence, and a permanent ceremonial platform had been built in front of it. This has saved some of the hard work previously needed to move wooden platforms into place before ceremonies. A further improvement was delayed until 2007, when a grant from the Faith Communities Capacity Building Fund has finally allowed the installation of a colourful new explanatory notice board, with paintings by Amina Inoue.

Looking back on my time at All Saints' I can see that reflection upon the experience of the worship there led us to avoid, as far as we could, any distinction between insider and outsider. We decided that as soon as anyone came into the building they were to be treated as an insider. The language of 'us' and 'them', so misleading and so divisive in western society today, had no place. So often acts of worship seem designed to *define* who the worshippers are, who is in and who is out. I believe that it is so much better to move beyond that approach and to strive for a way of working in which worship is understood as an effort to *create* a situation: a situation in which humans are drawn together so that their hearts may be warmed by an experience of the divine presence and their lives changed in response.

The imperative of inclusion had arisen from a practical approach to fragile urban worship. I say *fragile* because in the inner-city setting every act of worship has to be put together with painstaking but rewarding effort. The show must be 'put on the road' afresh each time. Careful attention must be given to the hinterland of worship, with all its facets, if inclusion is to be achieved. On further reflection it becomes clear that what started as a practical response will have far-reaching consequences. For example, when children are included in the worship they naturally come forward and hold out their hands for the bread at communion. 'Do not forbid them,' says Jesus. And who could with integrity turn the Buddhist monk away? If worship is understood to be an act of *creation* rather than of *definition*, then the receiving of bread and wine at the Eucharist is seen to be a sacrament of welcome, hospitality and inclusion, rather than a statement of adult membership, of us and them, as is often the case. Once we embark on the road to inclusion, it will not be long before the perception of baptism as the once-for-all gateway to every aspect of Christian life must come into question. Suppose a worshipper is moved to receive communion. Should baptism be at that crucial moment a prerequisite? If it is, then can there be any reality to our claim to be inclusive? Or if Muslim children are regular churchgoers, what message will our present approach to baptism convey to their family? A message, I submit, of conversion and separation. I do not believe that message to be a proclamation of good news in the present age.

Inclusive worship is mission; it is a primary way in which the Church takes its part in God's mission. The Church then no longer seeks to be the ark within which the few are kept safe from the flood: rather, it aspires to be part of the rainbow, signalling and making known in our tiny but still significant way that God's covenant is with all.

I am deeply grateful to Bhikkhu Nagase and others associated with the London Peace Pagoda that we were able to share sacred space together as neighbours and friends. My understanding of the Church's role and calling will never be the same again.

Response by Bhikkhu G. Nagase

As a monk of the Nipponzan Myohoji, I am dedicated to following the path initiated by our Founder and Preceptor, the late Most Venerable Nichidatsu Fujii. To my understanding, the friendship that the Revd Alan Gadd has described between All Saints' Church and the London Peace Pagoda is something that seems very natural to me in the light of our Founder's vision.

From a piece of his writing, we learn that our Founder believed that the project to build a Peace Pagoda in London was very important, though not everyone shared his view.

Completion of the Peace Pagoda in London by Nipponzan Myohoji is now within sight, and finance is not a problem. The meaning of this Pagoda is not easily understood by everyone in the Order. Some thought that we should not undertake this project, because of the shortage of money. In the future, after I have passed away, such an opinion may prevail in the Order, but remember that the people of London, who decided to build a Pagoda, probably grasped its significance in the fullest sense. In order to create world peace, we must focus on a central point where everyone throughout the world can be united.

Our Founder passed away in his hundredth year, on 9 January 1985. The London Peace Pagoda was completed and inaugurated on 14 May in the same year. Our Founder had expressed his delight that its completion was near, and had explained its importance in the following words, reproduced in a booklet for the inauguration:

Why is this encounter of Christianity and Buddhism so important in the twentieth century? Today's civilisation is based on materialism. The materialistic civilisation, using science as its tool, has been developing constantly, scientists being regarded as the leaders of the times. Most young people want to become scientists, but it is scientific developments which are leading us into the tragedy of the annihilation of humanity. Concerned about this, scientists have now begun to think that such a tragedy must be prevented by every conceivable means. But the road to prevention is not to be found in science, hence the scientists' dilemma.

Where is the solution to be discovered? It will not be found in today's scientifically oriented civilisation. The non-violent movement of Mahatma Gandhi was an expression of this. Many people of the world are now looking to his non-violent movement as their hope of being freed from the threat posed by the civilisation of science. The religious basis of the non-violent movement was laid as far back as more than 2,500 years ago, and seen in both Buddhism and Christianity, both religions being manifested in the form of the London Peace Pagoda.

Namu Myo Ho Ren Ge Kyo.

Further reading

Alan Gadd and D. C. Premraj (eds), 2001, *New Lamps: Fresh Insights into Mission*, London: All Saints' Church, Battersea, available from Alan Gadd, 24 Holmewood Gardens, London SW2 3RS.

Buddhism for World Peace: Words of Nichidatsu Fujii at Milton Keynes in 1979, 1980, translated by Yumiko Miyazaki, Tokyo: Japan-Bharat Sarvodaya Mitrata Sangha.

Note

1 A kaikyoge: a verse for opening the Lotus Sutra: www.nichiren-shu.org/nichirenshu_news/Nichiren157e.pdf.

12 Travelling Together

A journey to the Punjab, India

SARAH THORLEY

with a response by Gurbakhsh Singh Garcha

Have reverence for Christ in your hearts, and honour him as Lord. Be ready at all times to answer anyone who asks you to explain the hope you have within you, but do it with gentleness and respect.

1 Peter 3.15–16[1]

There is a Light that shines beyond all things on earth, beyond us all, beyond the heavens, beyond the highest heavens, the very highest heavens.
This is the light that shines in our heart.
All this universe is in truth Brahman.
Brahman is the beginning and end and life of all.
This is the Spirit that is in my heart, smaller than a grain of rice, or a grain of barley.
This is the Spirit that is in my heart, greater than the earth, greater than the sky, greater than heaven itself, greater than all these worlds.
This is the Spirit that is in my heart, this is Brahman.
To him shall I come when I go beyond this life.

Hindu scriptures: from Chandogya Upanishad 3[2]

The proposition

When information about a two-week study tour in the Punjab dropped on to my doormat, I jumped at the opportunity. The expedition was being arranged under the auspices of the

Lewisham SACRE (Standing Advisory Council for Religious Education). It was the inspiration of Gurbakhsh Singh Garcha, a Sikh councillor and chair of the SACRE. Gurbakhsh and Ruth, his (English) wife, were inviting council employees who worked in local schools or for other community projects with people from diverse religious backgrounds to stay in Ludhiana in the Punjab with his family and their neighbours.

The aim was to give us an experience that would deepen our understanding of the religious and cultural backgrounds of the people with whom we worked here in the UK and enrich us with a vision of inter faith relationships in a country where people of different religions have co-existed for centuries.

Seven of us went: Jane taught English as a second language to adults and was already a stalwart traveller. Cicelyn, from Grenada, was a mother of two, and working for Lewisham Council. Kirsty was a young, recently qualified teacher of religious education in a boys' secondary school. Blazena was a primary school head teacher, and her sister Janet a singer and university admissions officer.

Elizabeth, a close friend of mine, had just been accepted for ordination training in the Church of England: 'I wanted to find out as much as I could about the beliefs held by Sikhs and to meet them in the place which was the cradle of their faith. I was also hoping to clarify my own thoughts about the relationship of my Christian faith to other faiths.' After a week in India, she said to me, 'My theology is in freefall!'

Only Jane and I had been to India before.

The deal was that on our return we would all report back to our respective places of work and/or worship. Depending on our situations, we would speak about our experiences and their relevance to multi faith South London, put into practice what we had learned, and promote the idea of more inter faith exchanges.

Even though, living in South London, we were all used to a multi cultural and multi faith environment (except for Elizabeth who lives in rural Wiltshire), how many of us had actually been into a Sikh home? A Hindu temple? Spoken with a Muslim teacher? Or an Indian Christian? Or, indeed, who among us had invited a Sikh or Hindu to our home or church? We were about to embark on 'the India experience', encountering Sikh hospitality in particular and learning about the Sikh way of life as we never could have done otherwise.

The journey

Our flight to Delhi with Jordanian airlines gave us twenty-four hours in Amman on the way. On board, the direction of the Ka'aba in Makkah was displayed on the screen at regular intervals. Already we were being made aware of our multi faith world.

It was Good Friday and Elizabeth and I quietly read the Good Friday liturgy in our hotel room before setting off for Amman city centre. We enjoyed our bus ride with the locals, the lively Arabic music and the bus conductor puffing at his cigarette underneath the 'No smoking' notice on the bus window. The call to Friday worship echoed across the city and the prayers and sermon from the King Hussein Mosque were relayed into the nearby restaurants and cafés. Non-Muslims and women are not admitted to the mosque. Around the mosque, it was crowded with people. Some elderly characters wearing long white robes and the national red-and-white-check head scarves were in deep conversation around the washing fountain, but most men were dressed in dull western clothes. There were very few women around on the streets and as five western women we felt quite conspicuous; however, most people were friendly and we were often greeted with 'Welcome'. Scores of armed police, some with riot shields, lounged around the pavements, smoking. It was the day of an Arab peace summit on Israel/Palestine being held in Beirut, but Ariel Sharon was driving tanks into Ramallah to avenge the Passover suicide bombing three days earlier. Hence the high police presence.

Was this really, we wondered, to be an expedition where we would discover some 'good news' cross faith relationships? And would we be able to distinguish between what was politically or racially motivated strife and what really was religious dispute?

Our first three days in India were packed with visits to significant faith places in Delhi and Agra. Within hours of arriving we were being pedalled around in cycle rickshaws in the very heart of Old Delhi. It was April and already hot. Our cyclists strained and lurched through the bumpy, seething alleyways of Kanari Bazaar, crowded with booths selling every imaginable merchandise, some draped with scarlet and gold tinsel cloths for adorning the deities, others glittering with scarlet and gold wedding saris and jewellery and garlands – a blur of colour and light and noise and smells and human activity. Our destination was the cool marble of a small and beautiful Jain Temple hidden away at the end of an enclosed alleyway, where a clutch of boys were playing 'cricket' with a tennis ball and a young woman was ironing with a heavy old flat iron. The priest, wearing a loin cloth, showed us round the jewel of a temple, elaborately embellished with white marble and with silver images of their twenty-two Jinas (supreme spiritual teachers). Every inch of the walls and ceilings was covered with dazzling intricate paintings, silver inlay and carved marble pillars. Next stop was the Raj Ghat for a quiet reflective time at the simple black marble slab and eternally burning flame which is Gandhi's tomb in a garden beside the River Jumna. Then there was the Bangla Sahib Sikh Gurdwara, the Bah'ai Lotus Temple, the wondrous Taj Mahal in Agra and the deserted city of Fatipur Sikri. At the beautiful, white marble, lotus-shaped Baha'i Temple, the crowds of visitors are asked to maintain silence inside. Within the silence are intermittent readings from scripture, and Elizabeth was amazed to find herself listening to John's Gospel in such a 'foreign' setting. Readings from all the world's scriptures are read and valued in Baha'i teaching.

And in the middle of all this it was Easter. Elizabeth and I took a rickshaw to Saint James', the oldest church in Delhi, on Easter morning. Apart from us and the elderly presiding priest, it was an entirely Indian congregation. The service was an *Alternative Services Book* communion with all the familiar Easter hymns and a mass surge forward of the congregation to receive the sacraments. It was during the prayers that we learned that the Queen Mother had died the night before.

The Punjab

But it's time to move on to Ludhiana, the heart of my story. Ludhiana is a three-and-a-half-hour express train journey from Delhi. It is a big industrial city in the Punjab, where most of India's bicycles are made. Punjab is the land that gave birth to the Sikh religion through the teachings of Guru Nanak in the fifteenth and sixteenth centuries. In a nutshell, Guru Nanak, living in the north of India, which had been ruled by the Muslims since the invasions starting in AD 700, taught the best from the religions of Islam and Hinduism. He rejected many of the petty rituals of both religions, he rejected hierarchies and caste system, and he rejected forced conversions. He taught belief in One God and equality and freedom of belief for everyone: kings and labourers, men and women. Ik Oankar, the Gurmukhi letters for 'One God', are to be found in every Sikh home and gurdwara. Gurmukhi is the ancient language of the Sikh scriptures.

When the British partitioned India in 1947, an arbitrary line was drawn through the province of Punjab. Less than a third of the Punjab is now in India and the rest is part of Pakistan. In the terrible carnage of 1947 most of the Sikhs, along with Hindus, fled east to the Indian side as the Muslims fled west to the Pakistan side. Gurbakhsh, who was twelve years old at the time, told us of many heroic acts of courage as his grandfather and other Sikhs and Hindus tried to save their Muslim neighbours and smuggle them safely across the border, at great risk to their own lives. It has been a particular tragedy for the Sikhs to have had their homeland split in two, and often it has not been possible to cross the border from one side of the Punjab to the other. Many of the Sikhs' sacred sites, such as the birthplace of Guru Nanak, and Lahore from where Maharajah Ranjit Singh ruled his kingdom in the 1800s, are in Pakistan Punjab.

It's necessary to know at least this much of the history to understand how it is that the people relate to each other today. Today, the population of the Indian (east) Punjab is about 50 per cent Sikh and 40 per cent Hindu. The rest are Muslims, Christians and Buddhists.

Punj means five, *ab* means water; Punjab is the land of five great rivers which irrigate the land and make it a rich agricultural area. Therefore many of its inhabitants are farmers and the quantities of wheat grown have given it the reputation of the 'bread basket of India'.

Although Ludhiana is a big city and we saw shocking plastic-shelter slums on some of our excursions, the district where we were staying had a bustling small-town atmosphere. Ludhiana is not on the tourist route and we didn't see another white person for ten days. We experienced India from the inside, sharing the daily lives of our hosts: their food, prayers, shopping, excursions to friends and relatives in villages, and indeed the hardships of limited water and electricity cuts – it's tough in the heat, when the ceiling fans stop and the fridge goes off.

Our very first morning, we were woken by Hindu bhajans (hymns) jangling from the microphones of a local temple, soon to be complemented by the slower rhythmic echo of Sikh gurbani (sacred chanting) drifting over the flat concrete rooftops from the other direction. After breakfast we all launched out into the nearby 'high street' to buy dupattas, long scarves with which to cover our heads when we went into gurdwaras and mosques. The kilometre-long street was crammed with every imaginable 'shop', seething with every imaginable vehicle and resounding with every imaginable noise. The overloaded rickshaws, chugging, sputtering and tooting, competed for road space with multiple-passenger bicycles, motor bikes, trucks, ox-carts, donkeys, horse-drawn carts, mopeds, pedestrians, cycle rickshaws and buses, all in varying stages of dilapidation – oh, and the occasional private car.

We were very conspicuous and people stopped and stared in astonishment at us white-skinned foreigners (Cicelyn, from the Caribbean, was even more of a novelty); but the staring was not hostile and if we smiled we nearly always got a smile back.

The Sikh family experience

Our life in Ludhiana revolved around the home of Gurbakhsh's cousins, where he and Ruth were staying. Pritam is a quiet and dignified man with a white beard and turban and a warm smile, and his wife Kuldip is a sweet lady who embraced each of us as we arrived. With them lived their daughter Daisy, her husband Jatinder and their four-year-old daughter Josephine, and Pritam's kindly brother who was deaf and didn't speak much English. Pritam's and Kuldip's son Timpi was visiting from England with his English wife Rachel, and also staying was Itsuko, a Japanese friend of Daisy's. Various other cousins were in and out of the house most days. That extended network of family relationships and responsibilities made a great impression on me.

Elizabeth and I were staying next door with Gurdev Kaur, a charming widow, and her two teenage sons who were extraordinarily kind and generous in their welcome of two complete strangers into their home. The boys gave up their room for us and slept on a couch. There was a washing room, but water for only two hours twice a day. Because the weather was very hot, we didn't mind that there was only a slow trickle of cold water. I would stand under the tap, in a plastic bowl, treading underfoot my clothes that needed washing, as I washed myself and my hair. We learned about the value of water.

The single-storey house had a flat roof where I spent many contemplative hours watching the domestic activities going on in the surrounding narrow streets and back yards and on neighbouring rooftops and listening to all the sounds of traffic, voices, birds and animals. It was a good place to write a journal, from which much of what I am now writing is recollected. Sometimes the boys, Timu and Mickey, came up and chatted. I remember one conversation with Timu, who was seventeen, when I asked him if it had been a difficult decision to have his hair cut (traditionally devout Sikh men and women do not cut their hair). 'Yes, very difficult.' 'Do you go to the gurdwara?' 'Sometimes. My mother goes every day.' 'Is it not important to you?' 'God is important to me, but I don't need to go to the gurdwara. God is in here, in my heart.'

One evening Gurdev Kaur showed us her prayer corner in her bedroom with pictures of the Sikh Gurus and postcards of (Hindu) Lord Krishna and Ma Lakshmi. She told us she prayed the japji (morning prayers) there early every morning. I showed her my book of Guru Nanak's teachings and she read aloud the first part of the japji; then Elizabeth got out her Bible and we read together the beginning of John's Gospel. Meditation on the name of God was something we all understood. It was a lovely moment, sharing our sacred words. The japji begins:

> There is only One God : Whose name is Truth
> Who is without fear : Who is without hate
> Who is timeless and without form :
>   Who is beyond birth and death
> The self existent one : Who can be known by the Guru's grace.

The village experience

We were privileged to have two wonderful days visiting relatives and friends in nearby villages. The one-time headman of the first village was Gurbakhsh's lifelong friend. He and his wife greeted us in their home along with various other family members, first with cold drinks and later with a delicious lunch. As with most houses in which we were welcomed, it was sparsely furnished with little more than chairs and covered beds to sit on, a few cushions, a table and family photographs. In the back yard was a shed with their three buffalo, the mud oven where the chapattis are cooked, a mangle-like contraption which chops green alfafa for the animals, and rows of dung cakes drying out in the sun. The essentials of life.

Our hosts walked us along the dusty track through the rambling village. First stop was the tiny Hindu shrine to the god Shiva, which shares an entrance and a small shady courtyard with the simplest of Sikh gurdwaras – a room with the Sikh holy book beneath its canopy, a railing around it, an offering box and a mat in front. Here Hindus and Sikhs offer devotions at both shrines and the Sikh flag flies next to the small coned dome above the Hindu shrine. The largest building in the village was a gurdwara painted black and white. We learned that there were about 2,000 families in the village and seven gurdwaras.

We also visited the nursery school where there were about twenty-five Sikh and Hindu children (from several castes). Their equipment seemed to be a few wooden cut-out templates, three metal rocking boats, a wall chart showing different fruits, a Punjabi alphabet chart and a blackboard. They were growing onions in their garden. At the primary school we found boys and girls learning separately, all dressed in bright blue and sitting in neat rows on the ground with their slates and chalk. Some of them had paper and a kind of quill pen. The few books they had were very basic and worn, and the dual-language books and jigsaws and other supplies we had brought as gifts were opened with great ceremony and appreciation. I thought of the equipment and resources we have in our schools in the UK, and indeed what we throw away.

Excursions

Later that week we visited the prestigious KVM private school in Ludhiana. At the time of our visit, monthly fees of about £15 were paid by parents of 5,000 children aged five to eighteen. It is very exclusive. We were told that both parents are required to have university degrees (and it's been known for a father to borrow or pay for a woman with a degree for the admissions interview). Competition is high and children come from a wide area. Resources are impressive, standards very high and behaviour impeccable. We saw Hindu and Sikh pupils collaborating in a worship assembly. There were no Muslims in the school.

The same day we visited a Muslim school where the dedicated

teachers were catering for 600 local children with approximately £850 funding a year from the government – and that includes teachers' salaries. It is in a poor area and parents contributed about 28p a month, if they could afford to; however, we were told that no child would be turned away. About 60 per cent of the children were Muslim and the rest belonged to other religions. There was an hour a day given to Islamic studies, during which the non-Muslim children did general studies. About twenty of the older boys spend much of the day learning to recite the Qur'an by heart, and some of them will go on to become imams. Facilities are absolutely basic: no money for books, or for PE, art or science equipment, and up to sixty children in a class. One classroom, completely bare but for wood and metal desks and a blackboard, had on the wall a torn map of the world (with the British Empire still in pink) and a map of India drawn by a child with the words 'I love India' and 'God is One'. The children have to bring their own pens, pencils and exercise books. We had a quick whip-round: a donation that was much appreciated. I have kept in touch with the enthusiastic young headmaster and have sent out a few packages of resources. Education is seen as a most valuable asset: every child aspires to go to school, and teachers are highly regarded in India.

Still on that same day, we were taken to the Christian Medical College and Hospital which had been founded in the late nineteenth century by an English woman, Edith Brown. Three (Indian) chaplains talked to us about the training of nurses, half of whom were Christian (there are about 2,000 Christian families living in the locality). The College and Hospital evidently had a very high reputation and yet the chaplains told us they were awaiting with apprehension the outcome of a political debate about removing the control of institutions from minority religious bodies. We were asked to pray for a positive result. We had an interesting conversation about religious tolerance. We heard that intolerance and communal strife is often fomented by politicians for their own ends, but that most people at the grass roots live peaceably together. Britain was referred to in passing as 'post-Christian'!

I reflected that here in the UK, also, it's often the political agenda 'out there' that we hear about through the media that raises anxiety and engenders suspicion, that fosters stereotyping and prejudice and that can poison our grassroots relationships if we are not very careful. Trust begins to be undermined and it is so important not to let these outside factors control how we relate to each other as neighbours and friends with common concerns.

The pilgrimage experience

Two most wonderful and unforgettable pilgrimages were part of our itinerary. Travelling with Sikhs, for whom the places were so significant, gave the whole experience an extra, deeper dimension. The first pilgrimage was a fascinating cross-country drive north to the foothills of the Himalayas to Anandpur Sahib, where we stayed overnight in pilgrim accommodation next to a small gurdwara which had been funded and built by a Sikh community in Birmingham.

But for me our pilgrimage to the Harimandir, the Golden Temple in Amritsar, was the fulfilment of a dream and one of the seminal experiences of my life. I had researched and written about it for a schoolbook and now I was actually to go there. I wasn't disappointed.

Our bus tipped us out on the edge of the busy and bustling town of Amritsar and, with much excitement, gesticulation and bartering, our guide transferred all eighteen of us (Gurbakhsh's extended family had come too) into horse-drawn tongas to take us to the Golden Temple complex. It was an amazing fifteen-minute journey lurching through the din and the potholes of the absolutely chaotic narrow streets, missing by inches rickshaws and motorbikes, the odd car and a million bicycles. And then there it was, framed by the arch of the gateway, gleaming brilliant gold.

But first was a visit to Pingalwalla, which left me with indelible images. It is an orphanage-cum-refuge for all-age mentally disabled women. The caring work is directed by a most remarkable retired Sikh army officer who radiates compassion for these outcasts of society and inspires others to join in the difficult and dedicated work. As we walked around, many of the children ran up to the Captain to hug his legs or hold his hand, and he addressed each one of them so lovingly. The place had been founded by Bhagat Puran Singh, by all accounts a most saintly man who had died five years previously.

There could be no better place in which to reflect on all our experiences than in the serene peace of the marble cloister (parikrama) which surrounds the pool at the Golden Temple.

The whole scene was bathed in soft evening light, the Temple reflection shimmering gold on the water, and I spent an hour on my own there. I listened and watched and contemplated and gave myself to the strains of the voices chanting the words of the holy scriptures, to the soothing rhythmic sounds of the tabla (drums) and harmonium and to the atmosphere of sanctity and devotion. All around the wide, patterned marble paving people were quietly walking, sitting, praying or reading devotional books. It really is one of the most beautiful – in every sense of the word – places I have ever been. Most people were so friendly, acknowledging me (and staring quite a bit), smiling, and sometimes asking where I was from. I saw only two other white people. One family followed me in awed astonishment and I couldn't even win a smile from them until I said 'Sat Sri Akal' (the Sikh greeting) – and then the whole family wanted to greet me and shake my hand.

You can't visit a gurdwara without being fed in the langar. Hospitality is a key tenet of Sikhism. About 600 of us waited outside for the huge doors of the langar to open. All at once there was a terrific pounding of a massive drum, like thunder; the doors opened and we all poured in and sat down cross-legged in long lines. With speed and efficiency we were given stainless steel dishes, spoons, mugs and chapattis; dahl and beans were slopped from buckets into our dishes. Opposite us sat two ragged young street boys and a man wearing a smart orange turban with his wife and daughter: equality Sikh-style. We were curiosities but everyone was very friendly, and after eating we were allowed to go behind the scenes to see the huge cauldrons of bubbling dahl, the teams of volunteer men and women making chapattis and the chain of washers-up in a deafening clatteration of stainless steel. No dish-washing machines here.

We returned to the Golden Temple to sit by the water for half an hour before the evening ritual of putting the holy scriptures, the Guru Granth Sahib, 'to bed'. The golden reflection dazzled in the dark water and, as we watched, a crowd of pilgrims gathered round. Prayers were chanted, rose petals were thrown, and a long curved horn was blown as the holy book emerged, borne aloft on a cushioned palanquin with long poles, rather as we imagined the Ark of the Covenant might have been carried. It was taken ceremoniously into the Akal Takht building where it would rest for the night.

Our own 'rest for the night' was in nearby pilgrim lodgings, on mattresses on the floor, five to a room and with basic washing facilities. Sleeping on a hard 'bed' and washing under a cold tap helped me to identify slightly more with those sleeping on the street and washing under a communal standpipe. Perhaps that is one of the purposes of pilgrimage.

Kirsti and I were up at dawn to see the sun rise from the roof of the Golden Temple; there we sat and read from the book of Guru Nanak's teachings that I had brought.

I made one last foray into the surrounding bazaar with fellow teachers Blazena and Kirsti to buy Sikh artefacts to bring back for our schools: a turban length, pictures and posters of the Ten Gurus and the Golden Temple, the Ik Oankar, a jigsaw of the Punjabi alphabet, a langar dish and various other souvenirs.

I found it a most moving and involving experience to be with genuinely devout people at a time and place that means so much to them. My own spirit, my own connection with God, somehow felt expanded and I was living more fully, perhaps with more heart and less head.

Parties and farewells

Back 'home' in Ludhiana – and it really felt like coming home – there were only a couple of days left. The mehindi artists came one evening to adorn our hands with mehindi patterns (the intricate traditional patterns drawn on the hands and feet, particularly of brides). It was fascinating to watch the detailed designs materialise on the back of my hand, the henna paste being squeezed out through a nozzle like icing. It gave a whole new meaning to doodling and, once fixed with a sugar and lemon juice mixture, it lasts for up to three weeks. The children were riveted when I got back to school in Brixton.

One last and perhaps most profound moment of all was when I went into the nearby small Hindu temple. In the peaceful inner courtyard, I sat on the ground at the foot of a life-size image of Jesus hanging on the cross. I watched as a man touched the feet of Jesus, touched his own head and stood for a moment in prayer. The early morning sunlight bathed the images of Jesus and of the Hindu deities Hanuman, Krishna and Durga and of the Sikh Guru Nanak and of the Buddha, and I marvelled at the possibilities for unity and harmony (not union or unanimity) between human beings, whatever their religious upbringing. I felt how crazy it was that we fill our world with religious arrogance and strife. The germ of an idea began to grow. Here was an example not just of tolerance, but of embracing each other's ways without deserting our own ways. And more are surely to be found. How could we make known this good news in order to counteract the 'bad' religious news and act as an inspiration for those who are willing to make the effort and not lose hope? This humble little Hindu temple really set me thinking. Could other grassroots stories and instances of inter faith harmony be collected together? And here I am now, writing this and editing this book.

I shan't forget that hour, and a similar time the following morning, as I sat on the ground, watching the Hindu devotees coming and going, reverently offering their prayers and their flowers, fruit and coins. A stray dog wandered in. The smell of incense and the murmur of devout prayers wafted on the air. The leafy banana palm in the middle of the courtyard shades a small shrine to Hanuman and tiny sunbirds hover for the nectar from the hanging purple flowers, their feathers glinting metallic blues and greens in the sunshine. I wrote:

I sit at the feet of my Lord
of Bhagwan Jesus
I sit in the shady courtyard
of a small Hindu temple
I sit at the foot of Jesus on the Cross
And I know that God is One
I share God with this Hindu devotee
who touches the feet of Jesus
I share God with the old man praying
before Lord Krishna
I share God with the young mother
placing flowers before Matajji
I share God with the Sikh caretaker
of this Hindu temple
And I know that God is One
That we all belong to God
That God belongs to all of us
My Lord Jesus
looks down from his Cross with Love
and embraces us all
Brahman is indeed One

On our last night, they threw a street party for us. Matting was laid down in the narrow street outside the house and a pink and white satin awning was strung overhead. Trestle tables were laid up with food, fans and neon lighting, a dance floor and disco were all set up. The festivities began with a display of traditional martial arts. A troupe of young men and boys wielded their swords and sticks with much panache. I felt somewhat vulnerable sitting on the floor at the front – well placed for photographs, but what if one of those flailing weapons went flying through the air? No health and safety checks or risk assessments here – how liberating to live dangerously. Then on came the colourful national bhangra dancers with their infectious energy and rhythm. Soon we were all on the floor and the party took off. It was really good fun and finished with thank-you presentations and lots of clapping and hugging.

Next morning we were up at 5.15 to catch the train. It was a wrench to leave Ludhiana: they really had become our family in those ten days. Their family solidarity, their generous way of life and their values gave us a lot to think about. I hoped I would see them again, and indeed I have. Some of them visit England most years, so I have seen them here, and two years after that first visit I stayed three nights with them on my way north to the Himalayas. It was a wonderful reunion.

Back home

Back in England we were charged with reporting back to our various situations. Undoubtedly the study tour had educated each of us individually to better understand other religions as we encounter them in our different professions, and it expanded our horizons as to how people of different faiths might better relate to each other. For me, apart from being a wonderful 'holiday', the experience has affected me profoundly – perhaps not in very obvious ways, but implicitly in my reactions and responses in all aspects of my life: in my school work, my writing, my social life, my church involvement and my own spiritual journey. It heightened my awareness of what really matters in life – family relationships, hospitality, friendliness to the stranger, acceptance and even appreciation of those who are different, coupled with the need for basic education, employment and healthcare. The relative domestic simplicity we experienced – water, milk and its products (from the 'sacred' cow), locally produced food, shelter, and simple home furnishings – made a deep impression on me. In India, religion and consciousness of the Divine in all of creation is integral to every detail of existence: this is a powerful experience. Of course it is not all perfect in India. There is poverty, inequality, political strife, pollution, family problems, nasty people and other negative aspects, but I wanted to find and learn from all that was positive.

Unlike in India, here in the UK, as we grapple with the challenges, opportunities and joys of our multi faith scene, we are treading new territory. Although there have been people from other faiths here for centuries, they have not been numerous or conspicuous. In our now 'global world' we are all connected in one way or another with people of other faiths, and it's helpful to observe and learn from places that have been doing it for longer.

Kirsti collated an exhibition of information and photographs of our journey, which went on show in 'Wavelength' Deptford Library and then on tour in local schools. Blazena shared her experiences with staff and pupils at her school and added her purchases from Amritsar bazaar to the school RE artefacts. Jane wrote a journal and some poems and found that her reflections on the experience enriched her teaching of English to a diversity of adult students. During her three-year theological training, Elizabeth was able to challenge some assumptions and stereotypes and to contribute very relevant comments, with a confidence based on her experiences in the Punjab, that bore considerable weight. Since her ordination, she has been asked to be a member of a group to raise inter faith awareness in the Diocese of Salisbury.

I reported back to my SACRE meeting. I spoke at assemblies at school and added the artefacts that I had bought to our school's RE resources. And I was pleased to be asked to share some of my reflections at morning service in All Saints' Church, Battersea, where an author of two of the other chapters in this book, Alan Gadd, was vicar at the time.

Without the inspiration and generosity of Gurbakhsh, Ruth and their families in the Punjab, it couldn't have happened. There may have been only seven of us, but who knows how our experiences may have affected others and sown some seeds that we'll never know about.

Response by Gurbakhsh Singh Garcha

As a Lewisham councillor and a member of the Education Committee I was closely involved in setting up the statutory Standing Advisory Council for Religious Education (SACRE) and Agreed Syllabus Conference (ASC). SACREs are responsible for facilitating and monitoring the teaching of Religious Education in community schools and the ASC provides the curriculum. I chaired the SACRE from 1991, when it was set up, until 2005. Our community school pupils learn about the six major faiths of the world in order to understand the main beliefs, principles and methods of worship of their fellow citizens. In Lewisham we called this 'Learning Together Through Faiths'.

The initial idea of the Study Tour of the Punjab was the result of my conversation with Denise Chaplin, who was the RE advisor for Lewisham and a member of the SACRE. Since three of the six faiths, Hinduism, Sikhism and Buddhism, originated in India, we asked if some of our RE teachers and officers would like to see, first hand, how these faiths were practised in India. The response was enthusiastic in spite of the fact that it had to be self-financed.

Sarah has described accurately and beautifully her perception of Sikh beliefs and how her Christian faith related to other faiths. In our family three of us have native British wives and our family members were used to meeting and entertaining foreign relatives and their friends. However, in our first group in 1999 there were 18 of us, who were all distributed among our neighbours, both Sikh and Hindu, to live as guests for nearly two weeks. Ludhiana was a majority Muslim area for a long time before partition but they are now a small minority, although our family lawyer and orthopaedic consultant are both Muslims. On the second occasion, when we needed fewer beds, some of our neighbours complained at not being chosen as hosts. Punjab is not a tourist area and the presence of even one or two westerners is unusual. The sight of our group members shopping and having their hair done, getting on the buses and dropping in to our local temples, became very popular. They were often invited in for tea, and when they left we were often asked where they had gone. We had very positive reports from guests and hosts alike and some long-term relationships have been established as a result. All and any subjects were discussed and people found how common were their basic humanity and values. Customs were different, but interesting rather than divisive.

Religions were to a large extent seen to be culturally based and as different paths to a common goal, rather than to different destinations.

To worship one God, earn an honest living, and share food with their fellow citizens are three main tenets of the Sikh faith. Food in all Sikh gurdwaras is provided free to anyone of any faith, caste or creed. This is called langar and is an important part of any service. Anyone can attend and participate in the daily worship. Some members of the second group were able to see Hindus, Muslims and Sikhs paying homage at the grave of a Muslim holy man. This happens at several places in India. Hindus and Sikhs often celebrate their festivals together and inter-marriages are not uncommon. Except when communities are stirred up by unscrupulous politicians they live harmoniously, and hospitality is a noticeable Punjabi trait not exclusive to Sikhs.

This has been a learning experience for both sides and I feel privileged to be a part of it.

Further reading

Peter D. Bishop, 1998, *Written on the Flyleaf: A Christian faith in the light of other faiths*, Peterborough: Epworth Press.

Thich Nhat Hanh, 1996, *Living Buddha, Living Christ*, London: Rider, an imprint of Ebury Press.

Guru Nanak, 1997, *Select Sikh Scriptures*, vol. 1, compiled and translated by K. S. Duggal, New Delhi: UBS Publishers.

Eleanor Nesbitt, 2003, *Interfaith Pilgrims: Living truths and truthful living*, London: Quaker Books.

Rabbi Jonathan Sacks, 2002, *The Dignity of Difference: How to avoid the clash of civilizations*, London: Continuum.

Notes

1 Scripture taken from the Good News Bible in Today's English Version, Second Edition, Copyright © 1992 by American Bible Society. Used by Permission.

2 *The Upanishads*, 1965, London: Penguin, pp. 113–14

13 A Rich Tapestry

MALCOLM TORRY AND SARAH THORLEY

Then I saw a new heaven and a new earth; for the first heaven and the first earth had passed away, and the sea was no more. And I saw the holy city, the new Jerusalem, coming down out of heaven from God, prepared as a bride adorned for her husband. And I heard a loud voice from the throne saying,

'See, the home of God is among mortals.
He will dwell with them;
they will be his peoples,
and God himself will be with them;
he will wipe away every tear from their eyes.
Death will be no more;
mourning and crying and pain will be no more,
for the first things have passed away.'

Revelation 21.1–4

To you shall vows be performed,
O you who answer prayer.
To you all flesh shall come.

Psalm 65.2

We have woven a book that is a rich tapestry of good things happening. Above all, it is a hopeful book. We have been inspired by writing it, and we hope that you have been inspired by reading it. One of our authors said, 'It wasn't till I actually wrote it down that I really reflected on it and realised the full significance of what we'd done.'

Just as people of faith have been together and different in each of the chapters, so each chapter has contained messages both together and different. Although each author worked with no knowledge of what the others were writing, we have been interested and humbled to discern some clear common threads running through the whole book.

Starting from where we are. Engagement between people of different faiths seems most often to evolve from the situation in which we find ourselves. There are no standard formulae that we can apply in different places and at different times. The methods of engagement emerge from the people, situations and events of each time and place. The journey is often a slow one, and there are no quick fixes, although there are examples of how collaboration – or confrontation – can move faster in times of crisis. The slow journey, different each time, can lead us into new and unexpected forms of encounter. Some of the efforts recorded in this book are genuinely new: we are treading new territory, making mistakes, exploring other people's holy ground, and weaving new colours into the rich tapestry of multi faith activity.

Doing things together. We have found that by *doing* things together, people of different faiths and of none often engage most creatively with each other. Through organising events or a meal, making cross faith links, going on journeys, running projects, serving organisations and their people – through actively *doing* these things, we entered into and built relationships.

Planning together. As we have discussed our experiences we have realised the importance of planning *together* for joint projects, with all parties starting out with open minds and willing to learn and to adapt as we go along. We think it significant that every chapter in this book contains some element of people of different faiths planning collaboratively. We have found teamwork, clear communication, and mutual respect to be essential ingredients to aim for

Starting before a crisis. We have recognised the importance of building relationships across faiths *before* a crisis occurs. Whether it's bombings and the resulting islamophobia, the desecration of a synagogue, a pastoral emergency, or a regional casino; and whether it's a local emergency, or a national or international one with local repercussions – riots in Oldham, cartoons in Denmark, the invasion of Iraq, an earthquake in Kashmir – the bonds of friendship need to be strong enough to withstand the resulting tensions and suspicions. The channels of communication need to be there before the crisis happens. The place is here. The time is now.

Sharing sacred space. We have been surprised by the sheer diversity of multi faith situations in which we have found our-selves involved and by how many different ways there are of doing things. We have discovered, for example, that sacred space can be shared in a wide variety of ways: through one faith offer-ing hospitality to another and the invitation being reciprocated, or through different faiths sharing the same space, either to-gether (maybe in silence) or at different times.

Worship and prayer can be experienced together in imagina-tively different ways. It may be through members of one faith being present at and observing the worship of another faith; or, by agreement, through a degree of participation in another faith's worship. Or it may be through the collaborative planning and sharing of a joint act of worship such as a civic service, when the integrity of those present who are not religious must also be considered. And there are many variations on these themes.

We know that there is a range of opinion about what is possi-ble in the area of shared worship. We have found it important to be aware of what the expectations are of everybody involved and to listen carefully to all of the sensitivities, so that people don't unexpectedly find themselves in a situation in which they feel embarrassed or compromised. This is especially true of group visits where we have a particular responsibility if we are involved as a representative of our religion.

Unobtrusive activity. As we have studied one another's chap-ters, we have realised how hidden much of the work we record has been: a teacher teaching, a chaplain visiting, a journey under-taken, a group learning, a meal together. Occasionally multi faith work and relationships emerge into visibility: at a funeral, during a school visit, on a charity collection day or at a civic serv-ice – but often hardly at all. This suggests that there is a lot more such quiet, creative, multi faith activity going on than we might have thought or that might be guessed at from media coverage. We hope that our readers will find ways of bringing more good news inter faith stories to light in order to encourage others and generate both hope and inspiration.

Facing a secular world together. We have found that some of the same difficulties have cropped up for many of us. One of the ongoing challenges is that we live in a largely secular world, with attitudes to religion – Christian or otherwise – ranging from sympathetic and supportive, through indifferent and sceptical, to scornful and even obstructive (though sometimes obstruction comes from within our own faith communities). All of us work within institutions, or deal in one way or another with institutions, and this means that we might find ourselves trying to explain our religious beliefs and practices to some completely baffled council officer, hospital nurse, prison officer or teaching colleague who has little knowledge of or interest in religion. These are people who are receiving government directives to work with faith communities and to implement practices that lead to 'community cohesion'. We need each other.

Choosing for leadership. We are aware that leadership roles in multi faith activity are most often occupied by Christians and that this can cause concern to people of other faiths. In principle, most opportunities are available to anyone of any religion with the necessary abilities for the task; but in practice there is still some way to go. For example, a considerable complication is the way in which different faith communities choose people for representative roles and for such tasks as chaplaincy; another is differing expectations of 'priestly' roles in different faith communities; and yet another is the complex relationship in our society between religion and ethnicity.

There is a need for more confidence and trust to be developed, between all parties, so that there can be more even 'power sharing'. We have no easy solutions to offer, but we do know that a large part of the answer is in deeper learning about one another's cultures and about the different structures of our faith organisations, and in giving time to work through the issues together as they arise.

Meaning different things. Language sometimes contributes to misunderstanding. The very words 'chaplain', 'priest' and 'pilgrimage', for example, can mean different things in different contexts and can hold quite different meanings for Christians, Hindus, Jews, Buddhists, Muslims and Sikhs. The concept of a chaplain may be an entirely new one for some people. It helps if we do not assume an instant understanding of what we mean by a word, and if we are always prepared to talk things through to avoid being at cross-purposes.

Understanding women's status. Some of us have found it difficult to engage with women in some of the other faith communi-

ties, especially some Muslim communities, because of a perceived or actual seclusion or subordination of women. However,
the overt sexuality of western women and men, and indeed the
sexual explicitness in all forms of the media, is as difficult for
many Muslims as is, for western Christians, the more extreme
modesty and even repression of women in some Muslim communities (and in some other religious groupings). Many
Christians and members of other religions would like to see more
sexual restraint, and so would some Muslims like to see more
freedom of expression for all Muslim women. There are extremes
on both sides but it is unhelpful and wrong to judge and stereotype any religion on the basis of one group whose practice may,
in any case, be more to do with culture, or even politics, than with
religion. As we have found, there is a wide spectrum of practice
and of possibilities for communication, and more than one of our
stories demonstrates outstanding collaboration with Muslim
women who are in positions of leadership and authority.

Distinguishing between religion, ethnicity and culture. As we
experience the worship, social events and homes of people of
different faiths, we experience an often bewildering variety of
customs. As within Christianity, there is a huge range of practices within each religious tradition, whether it be bereavement
customs, customs at prayer or family customs at home. Practices
will be partly attributable to the particular strand of the religion
(Orthodox or Progressive Jew), and partly due to the part of the
world a person comes from (Pakistani or Algerian Muslim) and
many other historical and climatic factors (African or Scottish
Christian).

We have all become aware of the need to learn to differentiate
between what is religious tradition and what is cultural and
ethnic custom (and sometimes political pressure), and of the
importance of not comparing a religious teaching of one religion
with what is a cultural practice of another. We have also recognised that adherents of many religious traditions do not separate
'sacred' from 'secular' as tends to happen in western society.

Reconciling groups within the same religion. An additional
and creative new learning that we have discovered is the way in
which people from different branches of the same faith (including Christians) find themselves meeting each other in the 'multi
faith' context, when otherwise they might not. Such meeting may

come about because different groups within the same religion have to relate to each other if they want to be involved with some joint project; or they might find themselves invited to sit on the same committee (such as a multi faith forum, or a local council initiative for Holocaust Memorial Day). Sometimes that relating becomes deeper because what the two groups share becomes clearer to them in the presence of a very different religion. Sometimes the two groups start to relate positively to each other because old enmities appear to be the scandal that they often are, especially as, together with other faiths, they relate to a difficult and secular world.

Learning from others. We all find that we have learned from the people with whom we have engaged. We have learned about their religions, their customs, their communities, their theologies and their spirituality. Our similarities and differences will often appear in a sharp new relief, and a very different religious world will sometimes reveal corners of our own religious world that previously we had not troubled to explore. This learning has become part of our own personal spiritual journey. Through respectful listening and reflecting on what we learn, and through the challenge of explaining our own faith to others, we have come to a deeper and broader understanding of our own faith as Christians. In all of this, we have found ourselves learning, in all humility, new things about God from each other.

Relating uniquely. We have learned that relationships are vital. It's personal. Our engagement has not been the Christian faith engaging with the Sikh religion, with Islam, with Judaism, with Hinduism, or with Buddhism. Our engagement has been as Christians engaging with Sikhs, Muslims, Jews, Hindus, Buddhists, Baha'is, Jains, Zoroastrians, and others. Each of us represents a unique take on our own religion, so what we have experienced is unique engagements between our faiths. Every engagement is vital to the totality of relationships between the world's religions. That's quite a responsibility.

Enjoying it. A very pleasant realisation has been that we have all enjoyed – and continue to enjoy – our engagement with people of other faiths. In spite of difficulties and misunderstandings, we wouldn't have missed it for the world. Whether it's been planning shared worship, being chaplains together, attaching prayers to a rope, or going on a journey, our horizons have been broadened, our own faith deepened, our knowledge expanded and our hearts touched; we have been changed by the people with whom we have engaged and we wouldn't want it any other way.

People of all faiths are together and different in our now global society. We live in a fast-changing world and the faiths together face a society that is both secular and complicatedly religious. We can only do it together and we can do it best by cherishing and enjoying our differences.

To Christians reading this book we would say: Enjoy your Christian faith and relate yourself, along with the faith you love, to people of other faiths. To people of other faiths we would say: Enjoy your faith and relate yourself, along with the faith you love, to Christians. It can start with a cup of tea, or a chat in the shop, or a card at a bereavement, and it can take you into life-changing experiences and learning. Then you'll know what we mean by 'together and different'.

Appendix 1
Guidelines but not Blueprints

There is really only one essential guideline, and that is to communicate: to listen with an open mind, to observe carefully, to ask when you're not sure, and to be prepared to talk it through.

If you don't know how to address someone, if you aren't sure what to wear, if you're uncertain what food to offer or what is expected in a place of worship – don't avoid doing it; start by asking. There are some things that are certain: tobacco is never allowed in a Sikh gurdwara, and shoes are always taken off in a mosque . . . but there is such a huge variety of practice within each religion that it's possible only to give the most general of guidelines. There are no blueprints. You thought all Buddhists were vegetarian? Go to the Vietnamese Buddhist temple in South London and you will be given a meal with fish after the worship. In Tibet the meat of yak is eaten. You thought only Sikh men wore turbans? Some Sikh women do too. You really can't say 'All Buddhists do . . .' or 'All Jews say . . .' Of course, it's helpful to have some information before you start. There are good reference books to help,[1] and you might find the following Dos and Don'ts useful.

DO

Be conscious of your role: are you involved as an individual or as a representative of your faith community? Or as both?

Be hospitable: invite people to your home, to your church, to your festivals, and share food. It's safest to provide vegetarian food unless you know that your guests eat meat (which meat?). If there is a mixed faith gathering, label the food and provide soft drinks only. And accept hospitality from others – on their terms. At a Sikh langar, for example, we will be asked to cover our heads, remove our shoes, maybe sit on the floor (if we are able), and invited to eat their food and enjoy their hospitality.

Communicate: about food, dress, customs and culture. All faith communities are diverse and different parts of one faith tradition can have very different beliefs and customs. If you're not sure about someone's beliefs or customs then discuss it beforehand.

Cross boundaries: taking off your shoes as you walk on holy ground, treading uncharted territories. We have to feel our way, admit mistakes, be open minded, be prepared to listen, and be prepared to share our own truths and insights with open hearts.

Dialogue: in inter faith dialogue we listen and engage with an open mind, seeking common ground and recognising and respecting differences.

Discuss: customs, beliefs and ethics: your own and other people's.

Differentiate: between religion and culture. For example, in India, arranged marriage is the custom/culture for Christians as well as for Hindus, Sikhs and Muslims.

Distinguish: between joining in or taking part in the worship of another faith, and observing or being present at worship or prayer. It's important to be clear what you are being asked to do and not to join in inappropriately or to feel that your own integrity is being compromised. This is especially important if you are arranging visits for groups such as schoolchildren. It is perfectly possible to sit quietly at the back, being present at worship but saying your own prayers in the devotional atmosphere.

Identify: with other people's life journeys and how they've come to their religious convictions and practices.

Join in: as much as you can.

Listen: really listen, as that's the key way to find out about someone's religion.

Observe: others' ways of life, customs and religious traditions; and observe your own: for each of us behaves in particular ways, and to recognise that is half way to understanding the particularities of other people's ways of life.

Read: other people's scriptures and your own.

Share: your own faith with passion and integrity. People of other faiths will respect us for our beliefs and convictions.

Take: care with language: many English words are used to describe something in another religion and the meaning is only approximate. For instance: 'priest' can mean very different things to a Christian, a Hindu, or a Jew. 'Baptism' is a term often applied to the Sikh Khalsa ceremony, but it is very approximate. Much western misunderstanding of the Hindu concept of God comes from the use of the words 'gods and goddesses' applied to their 'murtis' or 'devatas' which don't really have an English equivalent.

Understand actions in places of worship: I need to know before I go into a Sikh gurdwara that kneeling and bowing my head to the ground in front of the Guru Granth Sahib, the Sikh holy book (or indeed before the Buddha in a Buddhist temple), is not worship of the book (or the Buddha). If I know that it signifies respect and reverence for the teachings contained in the book (or the teachings of the Buddha), then I can choose to make that action without feeling compromised. Joining in the prayer positions with Muslims, however, would be joining in their worship. The choice to join in, if invited, needs to be informed.

Work: together on projects and issues of common interest.

DON'T

Assume: because you can't know about somebody else's religious beliefs without asking them.

Avoid: dialogue with people of other faiths because you feel that you aren't an expert in your own religion. Be honest, and say what you believe, what you value, and how you live.

Be apologetic: or 'politically correct' about visible religious symbols – that is the secular agenda.

Compare: the worst you know of their religion with the best of your own.

Compromise: your own integrity.

Judge: someone else's religion from the standpoint of your own life experience.

Stereotype: e.g. 'all Hindus worship 3,000 gods', 'all Muslims follow Sharia law', 'all Christians pray to the Virgin Mary / baptise babies', 'everyone wearing a turban is a Sikh'. Sometimes the differences within one religion may be greater than those between religions, and people from the 'liberal' wings of the different religions may find more in common with each other than with the more fundamentalist branches of their own religious traditions.

Wander: too far from your own comfort zone or ask others to step over theirs.

Notes for a school visit

Below are extracts from the guidelines for schools planning visits to places of worship prepared by members of the Lambeth SACRE.

Expectations of behaviour and dress: there are certain expectations of behaviour and dress which must be observed. It goes without saying that pupils should be instructed to behave quietly and respectfully, as they are entering buildings that are 'holy ground' for the community concerned.

For some children, some places will be very different from anything they have experienced. 'Different' sometimes causes embarrassed giggles, so preparation is very important – head coverings, for instance, could be tried on in the classroom before setting off.

If packed lunches are taken, they should be vegetarian (except at churches).

Modest dress is appropriate on all visits.

Church and synagogue: no particular dress code required.

Mosque: arms and legs covered; females cover their heads. Wear comfortable clothes for sitting on the carpet. Shoes are removed (so clean socks!).

Hindu and Buddhist temple: comfortable clothes for sitting on the carpet. Shoes are removed.

Sikh gurdwara: comfortable clothes for sitting on the carpet. Males and females cover their heads (coverings can usually be borrowed at the gurdwara). Shoes are removed. No cigarettes or alcohol are allowed on the premises.

Be aware ...

1 **Don't stereotype.** Your visit to 'a' Hindu temple will give the pupils a flavour of a Hindu temple. There is a huge variety of temples and wide variation of practices and beliefs within every religion. If you visit the Jamyang Tibetan Buddhist Centre in Kennington and the Japanese Nipponzan Buddhist Temple in Battersea Park, you'll find that there are differences, just as you will find differences if you visit St Leonard's C. of E. and Lewin Road Baptist churches in Streatham. Don't say 'All Hindus believe . . .' or 'All Christians do . . .'.

2 **Titles.** Do ask your contacts how they like to be addressed (by you and by the pupils) – Mr, Mrs, Reverend, Father, Imam, Rabbi, Brother, Sister, Bishop or first name.

3 **Photography.** Ask beforehand about taking photographs.

4 **Double check.** Phone the day before to confirm the visit. Occasionally events such as a funeral will mean that a visit has to be rescheduled.

5 **Preparation and follow-up.** Think about preparation lessons – what vocabulary would help the pupils understand features of the building, basic beliefs and worship practices.

Consider suitable follow-up work.

6 **Donations.** A donation should be made (not less than £1 per child is suggested). People are very generous about giving up their time to welcome schools (for example, a guide at one place of worship is a cab driver, so he is losing his fares); there's also the cost of heating and lighting, and refreshments may be provided.

A bunch of flowers is a nice gesture. At a Sikh gurdwara, a bag of sugar or flour or pasta for the langar is appreciated.

7 **Prepare parents.** Encourage parents to accompany you on the visit. It is of great benefit if they are able to discuss the visit with their child afterwards.

If there are children in the class of the faith community to be visited, consider asking their parents or grandparents to come into school and help with preparatory lessons and follow-up.

Remember, parents do have the right to withdraw their children from Religious Educational visits, but often they can be reassured, if the purpose and programme is carefully explained.

Finally be prepared to go with the unexpected! If the opportunity suddenly arises to observe prayer or meet a group . . .

However, it is advisable to establish beforehand, with all concerned, that these are educational visits and that the pupils would not be expected to take part in any worship activities. The distinction between 'taking part' and 'being present at' is important.

Note

1 See John Bowker, 1999, *The Oxford Dictionary of World Religions*, Oxford: Oxford University Press; and *Faith Directory: Religions in the UK*, available from the Multi-Faith Centre, University of Derby, Kedleston Road, Derby, DE22 1GB. Phone: 01332 591285. Email: mfd@derby.ac.uk.

Appendix 2
Resources

Rumman Ahmed, Doreen Finneron, Steve Miller and Harmander Singh, 2006, *Tools for Regeneration: Practical Advice for Faith Communities*, revised and expanded edition, London: The Faith Based Regeneration Network UK.

John Bowker, 1999, *The Oxford Dictionary of World Religions*, Oxford: Oxford University Press.

Barbara Butler, 2006, *Living with Faith: Journeys towards trust, friendship and justice*, Peterborough: Inspire.

Siriol Davies, 2007, *An Evaluation of Different Models of Inter Faith Activity*, London: South London Inter Faith Group.

Alan Dinham, 2007, *Priceless, Unmeasurable? Faiths and Community Development in 21st Century England*, London: The Faith Based Regeneration Network UK.

Faith Directory: Religions in the UK, Derby: University of Derby; available from the Multi-Faith Centre, University of Derby, Kedleston Road, Derby, DE22 1GB. Phone: 01332 591285. Email: mfd@derby.ac.uk.

Faith Meeting Faith: Ways forward in inter-faith relations: A resource for individuals and groups, 2004, London: The Methodist Church.

Inter Faith Organisations in the UK: A Directory, 2007, London: Interfaith Network for the UK: available from the Inter Faith Network for the UK, 8a Lower Grosvenor Place, London SW1W OEN, ifnet@interfaith.org.uk.

The Local Inter Faith Guide: Faith community co-operation in action, London: The Inter Faith Network UK with the ICRC, available from the Inter Faith Network for the UK, 8a Lower Grosvenor Place, London SW1W OEN, ifnet@interfaith.org.uk.

Sarah Thorley, 2004, *Talking Together: Conversations about religion*, Ropley: John Hunt Publisher.

Sarah Thorley, 2007, *Improved Understanding of South London's Multi Faith Situation*, London: South London Inter Faith Group.

Andrew Wingate, 2005, *Celebrating Difference, Staying Faithful*, London: Darton, Longman & Todd.

Appendix 3
Glossary

The following is a list of religious terms used in the book, with readers of different religions (or none) in mind. The definitions may refer to the context in which the words have been used. There is a bias to the context of this country and within the Christian context there is a bias towards Anglican terminology (most of the authors of this book are Anglican). Italics indicate that a term has its own Glossary entry

Abrahamic Looking back to Abraham as a spiritual ancestor: thus *Judaism*, *Christianity* and *Islam* are Abrahamic faiths. The story of Abraham (Abram to Jews; Ibrahim to Muslims) and his faithfulness to God, in the second century BC, is recorded in the book of *Genesis*

Acts [of the Apostles] A book of the *New Testament* in which *Luke* tells the story of the early *Church*. 'Apostle' is an early Christian title for *Jesus*' twelve *disciples* and for other authoritative *missionaries*

Adhan/Azan (Arabic) The Muslim call to prayer (five times each day)

Advent (Christian) The four-week season of spiritual preparation leading up to *Christmas*

aisle (Christian) The gangway between rows of pews (wooden benches) or chairs in a *church*

All Saints' Church/Day (Christian) Many *churches* are named after *saints* or 'All Saints'. All Saints' Day is an annual celebration of the saints (on 1 November in the west)

Allah and 'Insha-Allah' (Arabic) God and 'God willing' used by all Muslims and by Arabic speakers of whatever faith, to refer to God

Alternative Services Book (ASB) (Christian) A book of services for the *Church of England* published in 1980. The services are 'alternative' because the Book of Common Prayer remains in theory the normative liturgy of the Church

Andrew (Saint) Andrew was one of Jesus' first *disciples* and is the patron *saint* of Scotland

Anglican The Anglican Communion consists of all those *dioceses* worldwide that are in communion with the *Archbishop* of Canterbury: the diocesan *bishops* are invited to attend the Lambeth Conference, a consultative conference that occurs once every ten years

Angulimala Association (Buddhist) The Buddhist prison *chaplaincy* organisation: www.angulimala.org.uk

antiphon (Christian) In the western *Church*, sentences – usually from the *Bible* – said or sung before a reading, *psalm* or *canticle*

anti-Semitism Prejudice, violence or insult against Jews

archbishop (Christian) A senior *bishop*

archdeacon (Christian) A senior *priest* who is also a *bishop*'s assistant, with legal and other duties, in a particular geographical area

Ark (Jewish) (1) The boat Noah built to escape from the flood recorded in the book of Genesis; (2) the Ark of the Covenant, in which (according to the book of Exodus) the tablets of the Ten Commandments (see also *Judaism*) were kept and transported; (3) thus the place in the *synagogue* where the scrolls of the *Torah* are kept

Ash Wednesday (Christian) First of the 40 *penitential* days of *Lent*, leading up to *Easter*. At the Ash Wednesday *Eucharist* a *cross* is marked in ash on the worshipper's forehead as a symbol of mortality and penitence

Baha'i A religion founded by Baha'u'llah in the 1860s. Recognising the founders of all the major religions as 'Manifestations' [of God], its followers are active in *inter faith* work

baptism (or christening) (Christian) The *sacramental* ceremony, using water that has been blessed, for infants or new adult followers of *Jesus Christ*

Baptist A large worldwide Christian *denomination* in which there is an emphasis on *mission* and only adults can be *baptised* (at a 'believer's baptism')

benefice (Christian) A *parish* or parishes of which a *priest* is *incumbent*

Bhagwan (Hindu) 'Lord' – a devotional name for the deity (God)

bhajan (Hindu) Devotional song (*hymn*)

bhikkhu (Buddhist) The word, in many parts of the world, for a Buddhist *monk*; *nuns* are 'bhikkhuni' (Pali language)

Bible (Christian) For Christians, their scriptures including the books of the 'Old Testament' and the 'New Testament'. See also *Hebrew Bible* and *New Testament*

bishop (Christian) A senior *church* leader. In the *Anglican* Church, the bishop acts as a focus of unity and authority in a *diocese* and has *pastoral* care for its people and *clergy*

Blessed Virgin Mary An honorary title applied to *Jesus*' mother Mary. She is also recognised by Muslims as the virgin mother of Jesus and known as Mariam

Brahman (Hindu) The *Sanskrit* word for the Absolute, the One Supreme All Pervading Spirit (God). (Not to be confused with Brahma, the creator deity, nor with Brahmin – a member of the 'priestly' varna or *caste* of Hindu society)

The Buddha Means 'the Enlightened One'. Buddhism began with his teaching in the fifth century BC in India. He taught a (non-theistic) way of thinking and living, by *meditation* and seeking of the Truth, leading to enlightenment and freedom from life's suffering

canticle (Christian)   Song or prayer from the *Bible* used in Christian worship

caste (Hindu)   In Hindu society for thousands of years there have been four 'varnas' within which are hundreds of castes that designate a person's (inherited) position and occupation. There are now laws in India against discrimination on the basis of caste

cathedral (Christian)   The central (usually very large) '*church*' of each diocese in which the diocesan *bishop* has a 'cathedra' (a throne or seat)

catholic (Christian)   In the historic *creeds* the word means 'universal'. See also *Roman Catholic*

chador (Muslim)   Full-length cloak worn by women (Persian origin)

chalice (Christian)   A large goblet, often silver or silver plated, from which wine is received by members of a *congregation* at a *Eucharist*

chancel (Christian)   The (usually) eastern end of a *church*; the part of the building from which the *priest* leads the worship

chapel   A place for prayer

chaplain   Someone fulfilling a *pastoral* role in an institution, usually a hospital, factory, prison, university, etc. A chaplain is often, but not necessarily, an *ordained priest*; there are also *lay* chaplains

cheder (Jewish)   *Synagogue* school for Jewish children

Christianity   The religion, with its foundations in *Judaism*, established by the followers of *Jesus Christ* nearly 2,000 years ago

Christmas   Celebration of the birth of *Jesus* on 25 December in the western *Church* and on 6 January in the Eastern *Orthodox Church*

church   (1) a *congregation* of Christians; (2) the building in which a congregation meets; (3) the Church (note capital letter) means the entire universal body of Christian believers and all of its local manifestations; (4) also used as part of a *denomination*'s title, as in '*Methodist* Church'

Church of England (C of E)   The *dioceses* in England which have *bishops* in *communion* with the *Archbishop* of Canterbury. It has been the *Established Church* in England since 1534

'Churches Together'   A nationwide organisation of groups of *churches* of different *denominations* which promote Christian unity through collaborative discussion and activities in their localities

churchwarden (Christian)   Each *C. of E. parish* has two churchwardens elected annually. They represent the people of the parish and share with the *incumbent* the responsibility for the functioning of the parish and the maintenance of the *church* building

clergy (Christian)   A collective noun for *bishops, priests, deacons, ministers* and *pastors*, etc.

clerical robes (Christian)   Clothing worn by *clergy* during *church* services

commendation   At a funeral, the final words of farewell before the *committal*

committal   The words that commit a body to burial in the ground or to cremation in the fire

Common Worship **(Christian)**   The collection of alternative services authorised for use in the *Church of England* in 2000

communion (Christian)   When worshippers share bread and wine (recalling Christ's death on the cross) at the *Eucharist*. The service is also known as Holy Communion, the Lord's Supper or the *Mass*.

confirmation (Christian)   Confirmation in the *Anglican* Church is a ceremony expressing God's 'confirmation', as members of the Church, of people who were baptised as infants and who now, by their own choice, 'confirm' the promises made then on their behalf. If an adult is baptised, confirmation may follow immediately. (There is currently some debate as to whether someone may receive *communion* without being confirmed)

congregation   A gathering of people for the purpose of worship

convent (Christian)   A place where *nuns* live

conversion   To change from one religion to another or from no religion to belief. Some groups of some religions actively seek to convert people to their beliefs

Corinthians [Letters to the]   Two letters in the *New Testament* written by *Paul* to the *church* at Corinth

creed   The formal declaration of beliefs of a particular religion

cross (Christian)   Symbol of *Christianity* – because Christians believe that *Jesus* made the supreme sacrifice for humanity when he was put to death on a cross

crucifixion   A Roman punishment: a person was hung on a *cross*, a large upright stake with a crosspiece, which results in asphyxiation

curate (Christian)   Assistant priest, usually newly ordained

Damascus [road to]   The road from Jerusalem to Damascus on which *Paul* (the author of several of the letters in the *New Testament*) had a *conversion* experience after which he stopped persecuting Christians and became an ardent Christian himself

deacon (Christian)   The word means 'one who serves'. In the *Anglican* Church, deacon is the first of the threefold order of ordained ministry: deacon, *priest* and *bishop*. Most deacons serve for a year before a second *ordination* as priest. Some remain as lifelong deacons

deity   A god or goddess

denomination   A branch of a major religion, having the same basic beliefs but varying interpretations and modes of expression (often with centralised organisation)

desecration   Vandalism or other activity insulting to the *sacred* character of a place or object

devata (Hindu)   Lesser gods and spirits especially associated with Indian village life

diaspora   A scattering of religious people away from their spiritual homeland; used particularly of the dispersion of the Jews all over the world after the destruction of the *Temple* in Jerusalem by the Romans in AD 70

diocesan missioner (Christian)   A senior *priest* in a *C. of E. diocese* whose job it is to encourage the *parishes* to engage in *mission*

diocese (Christian)   A geographical area and its *parishes* with central administration for functions such as legal, *pastoral* and *spiritual* injunctions and the payment of *clergy*. The chief *pastor* of a diocese is its *bishop* (who might be assisted by area or 'suffragan' bishops). There are 43 *Church of England* dioceses in England and 13 more in the *Anglican Churches* of Scotland and Wales. There are 30 *Roman Catholic* dioceses in England, Scotland and Wales

Diocese of Southwark (Christian)   The *C. of E. parishes* of South London and of parts of Kent and Surrey. There is also a *Roman Catholic* Diocese of Southwark

disciple   A follower of a teacher, *prophet* or *guru*

Divali (Hindu/Sikh)   Major Hindu festival of lights lasting four to five days in October or November. The focus varies in different parts of India. Lakshmi, the goddess of prosperity, is worshipped and the triumph of good over evil in the ancient story of Rama and Sita is celebrated. Sikhs also celebrate Divali, recalling events from Sikh history

Easter (Christian)   The most important Christian festival. The celebration of *Jesus' resurrection* – rising from death to life

Easter Dawn Liturgy   A *liturgy* (usually of readings and *Eucharist*, and maybe *baptism*) at dawn on Easter Day

Ecumenical Borough Deans   In London boroughs and elsewhere, each Christian *denomination* may appoint a Borough Dean to represent them at regular consultative meetings with members of the local authority and other parts of civil society

ecumenism (Christian)   The relating of different Christian *denominations* to each other at local, regional or national level to seek deeper unity

Eid (Muslim)   Means 'festival'. Eid-ul-Adha is celebrated at the end of the annual *Hajj* and Eid-ul-Fitre at the end of *Ramadan*, the month of *fasting*

Ephesians [letter to]   A letter in the *New Testament* written by *Paul* to the *church* in Ephesus

Epiphany (Christian)   The celebration on 6 January of the wise men's visit to the child *Jesus*. In the Eastern *Orthodox Church* this is when *Christmas* is celebrated

Established Church   In England, the *Church of England*, and in Scotland the Church of Scotland. The term recognises the somewhat anachronistic entanglement of the *Church* with the state

Eucharist (Christian) A fourfold action of taking bread and wine, giving thanks over them, breaking the bread, and sharing the bread and wine, imitating *Jesus'* actions during a meal with his *disciples* on the night before he died. The word's meaning generally extends to the whole act of worship, including *hymns*, readings, prayers, etc.

Evangelical (Christian) Evangelical Christians are distinctive in their ardent wish to 'spread the *gospel*' and they may take the words of the *Bible* very literally. Emphasis is on personal *conversion* and relationship with *Jesus* and the power of the *Holy Spirit*. Worship is often informal and exuberant

evangelist (Christian) Someone who tells the good news of *Jesus* and of the coming of the *Kingdom of God*. The word refers specifically to the authors of the four *Gospels*: *Matthew*, *Mark*, *Luke* and *John*

Ezekiel A Hebrew *prophet* and book in the *Hebrew Bible* (Old Testament)

Faith Communities Capacity Building Fund (2006–8) Money granted by the Government, and administered by the Community Development Foundation, to promote *multi faith* awareness and activity and improved governance and other skills among faith communities

faith school A school primarily for children of a particular religion with the aim of maintaining and fostering the spiritual ethos and moral values of that religion

fasting Going without food (and in some cases drink) for a period of time for religious reasons. A practice common to all religions to a greater or lesser degree

Fatima (Muslim) Daughter of the *Prophet Muhammad*

Five Ks (Sikh) The five symbols worn by devout Sikhs. The Punjabi word for each symbol begins with the sound of the letter K

Free Church This term generally refers to the main Christian *denominations* other than the *Church of England*, *Roman Catholic* and *Orthodox Churches*, such as the *Methodist*, *Baptist* and *United Reformed Churches*. There are other non-affiliated *congregations* which can be regarded as 'free churches' in their own right

Genesis [the book of] The first book of the *Hebrew Bible* (the Old Testament to Christians) containing stories of the creation and of heroes and otherwise of ancient Israel

Gentile (Jewish) A non-Jew

George (Saint) (Christian) The patron *saint* of England. Legend has it that George lived during the first or second centuries AD and that he slew a dragon. His courage was an important inspiration for the crusading Christian armies of the twelfth century

Golden Temple (Sikh) More correctly called the 'Darbar Sahib' or the 'Harimandir', it is the most *sacred* place for Sikhs and they visit it whenever possible. It was built in the sixteenth century in Amritsar in the Punjab, and the book of the holy scriptures, the *Guru Granth Sahib*, was installed at its centre. Later the building was completely covered with gold

Good Friday (Christian) The Friday before *Easter* Sunday, when the *crucifixion* of *Jesus* is commemorated ('Good' because what follows from Good Friday is seen as the triumph of good over evil and the means of salvation)

Gospel (Christian) (1) The good news of *Jesus Christ* and of the coming of the *Kingdom of God* which he proclaimed; (2) A book in the *New Testament* containing this good news. There are four versions of the Gospel – according to *Matthew, Mark, Luke* and *John*

grotto A cave or basement, often with a stream or pool, where a *saint* or *sacred* object is venerated

gurbani (Sikh) *Sacred* text written by the *Gurus*, often expressed as devotional songs or chanting

gurdwara (Sikh) The building where the *Guru Granth Sahib* is kept and where Sikhs meet for worship

Gurmukhi (Sikh) The script in which the *Guru Granth Sahib* is written. It means 'from the mouth of the *Guru*'

guru A *spiritual* teacher. To Sikhs it means one of the ten Sikh *Gurus* (and is spelt with a capital G)

Guru Granth Sahib (Sikh) The holy book of the Sikhs containing the teachings of the *Gurus*, treated with the greatest reverence as 'the living words' of the Gurus. Also called the Adi Granth

Guru Nanak (1469–1539) (Sikh) The founder of the religion which became *Sikhism*, in north India. He devoted his life to teaching about the One God and the equality of all people and to conciliation between Muslims and Hindus

Hajj (Muslim) The annual pilgrimage (which may take up to fourteen days) to *Makkah* in Saudi Arabia. All Muslims are required to make the pilgrimage at least once in their lifetime, if they are able to

halal (Muslim) It means 'allowed' ('haram' means 'forbidden') and most commonly refers to food – hence a 'halal' butcher produces meat from animals slaughtered according to Islamic law. Halal financial products are non-usury based

Hebrew Bible (Jewish/Christian) A collection of Jewish *sacred* texts: the *Pentateuch* (or *Torah*), the *prophets* and other books including *Psalms* and Proverbs. Approximately the same as the section of the Christian *Bible* known as the 'Old Testament'

hijab (Muslim) Modest clothing worn by many Muslim women, usually including a scarf to cover the hair and neck

Hinduism The religion of the majority of India's population, which has its origins in the Indus Valley civilisation of around 4000 BCE

Holocaust Or 'Sho'ah', meaning 'calamity' in Hebrew. The systematic extermination of the European Jews by Nazi Germany 1933–45 (and of other groups including gypsies and homosexuals)

Holy Communion (Christian)   See *Eucharist*

Holy Spirit   In *Christianity*, the third 'person' of the *Trinity* (see also next entry)

Holy Trinity (Christian)   During the first three centuries of the Christian tradition God came to be thought of as both one and three: as one God, and also as God the Father, who created the world; as God the Son, who became human in *Jesus Christ*; and as God the *Holy Spirit*

hymn   A devotional song

iftar/iftaari (Muslim)   The daily breaking of the *fast* at sunset/dusk during the month of *Ramadan*

Ik Oankar (Sikh)   Gurmukhi script meaning 'One God'   ੧ਓ

imam/Imam (Muslim)   (1) The man who leads the *congregational* prayers in a *mosque*, he is usually theologically educated (but not 'ordained' – not a *priest*); (2) For *Shi'a* Muslims, Imam (note capital I) has a particularly significant status and is the title of the immediate successors of the *Prophet Muhammad*

'Incarnate Word' (Christian)   *Jesus* understood as a word spoken by God having come in the flesh. ('Incarnation' is also used to describe Hindu manifestations or 'avatars' of God on earth)

incense   Resin or other substances which, when burned, give off smoke and a strong scent. Used in worship particularly by the *Roman Catholic* and Eastern *Orthodox* branches of *Christianity* and by Hindus and Sikhs, and also by Buddhists in their devotions to the *Buddha*

incumbent (Christian)   The *priest* responsible for the *pastoral* care of a *benefice* (a *parish* or group of parishes) and for its *church* buildings

industrial chaplain   A *chaplain* in an industrial institution. Many Christian industrial chaplains undertake a variety of additional activities in connection with the *Church*'s relationship to the economy

inter faith   Understanding, dialogue and engagement between people of different religions. See Chapter 1

intercessions   Prayer or petition on behalf of others: e.g. praying for those who are sick or dying

Islam   The religion derived from the teaching and leadership of the *Prophet Muhammad* (570–632 CE) and from the revelation mediated through him, in the *Qur'an*. The meaning of 'Islam' is: 'peace and security with God through allegiance and surrender to him'

Islamic Centre   An institution attached to the *mosque*, often in the same building and often indistinguishable from it organisationally, for the promotion of Islamic education and social life

islamophobia   Discrimination, intolerance or hostility towards *Islam* and Muslims

Ismaili (Muslim)   Historically a branch of *Shi'a Islam*. They give allegiance to a living *Imam* – the Agha Khan, whose family claims descent from the *Prophet Muhammad*. They are noted for their esoteric teaching and their charitable educational, social and health enterprises throughout the world

Jain   An ancient Indian religious and philosophical tradition. Jains follow the guidance of 24 great teachers (Jinas), the last and most famous of whom is Mahavira, a contemporary of the *Buddha* in the fifth century BCE. One of their central principles is 'ahimsa' (non-violence). There are about 25,000 Jains in Britain

japji (Sikh)   A sacred poem composed by *Guru Nanak* and recited by devout Sikhs as part of their daily morning prayers

Jesus Christ   A Jewish religious teacher who lived 2,000 years ago in Palestine. He healed the sick and taught in the name and in the power of God. His followers believed him to be the 'Messiah' (saviour) for whom the Jews were waiting. After he was *crucified*, his disciples experienced his miraculous rising from the dead. Christians believe him to be both human and divine. He is revered by Muslims as a *Prophet* of God (but not the 'Son of God')

John (Saint)/John's Gospel   John was one of *Jesus'* twelve *disciples*. The fourth *Gospel* is named after him, as are maybe three letters and the book of *Revelation* in the *New Testament*

John Wesley (1703–91)   An *Anglican priest* who became a passionate *evangelist* and itinerant preacher and founded the *Methodist* movement

Judaism   The history of the Jews and their relationship with God is revealed in the *Hebrew Bible* (the first five books of which comprise the *Torah*) and in the 'Oral Torah' or 'Rabbinic Literature' (e.g. the Mishnah and the Talmud). Moses was a key figure, leading the Jewish people (Israelites as they were called) out of slavery in Egypt and receiving the 'Ten Commandments' from God in about 1500 BC. Judaism is the foundation of both *Christianity* and *Islam*

Jum'a/Jummah (Muslim)   The weekly gathering of Muslims on Friday for midday prayer and sermon (*Khutba*)

Ka'aba (Muslim)   Arabic for 'cube'; the cube-shaped building that stands in the Great *Mosque* in *Makkah* in Saudi Arabia. Muslims worldwide face towards the Ka'aba when they pray and circle it seven times when they go on pilgrimage (*Hajj*) to Makkah. Traditionally it goes back to the time of *Abraham*

Khalsa (Sikh)   Means 'the pure ones'. Instituted by the tenth and last *Guru*, Guru Gobind Singh, in 1699, the Khalsa 'fellowship' is made up of those Sikh men and women who choose to make a particular commitment to the Sikh way of life, through a special initiation ceremony

khutba/khutbah (Muslim)   The sermon delivered by a Muslim teacher at Friday Prayer

Kingdom of God (Christian term)   The world as a place of justice and peace over which God reigns supreme, which *Jesus* came to herald and for which Christians strive. Jesus told parables (stories to make an important teaching point) about the Kingdom, which is future and to some extent present

kirpan (Sikh)   One of the *'Five Ks'*: a short steel sword worn by devout (*Khalsa*) Sikhs, signifying the Sikh commitment to justice

kosher (Jewish)   Food permitted to Jews according to the Jewish law in the *Pentateuch* and related traditions. *Orthodox* Jews observe these dietary laws more strictly than *Reform* and *Liberal* Jews

Krishna (Hindu)   One of the most popular of the Hindu deities, often worshipped with his consort Radha. He is the central figure of the famous epic poem The Bhagavad Gita, one of the most important Hindu sacred texts

laity/layperson   In the Christian tradition, all *baptised* Christians who are not in *ordained* ministry. In Buddhism, all Buddhists who are not *monks* and *nuns*: they have a religious duty to support monks and nuns in practical ways (for example with food and medicine)

langar (Sikh)   The kitchen and free (vegetarian) meal offered to everyone at a Sikh *gurdwara*. This hospitality is a fundamental feature of the Sikh religion

Lent (Christian)   A *penitential* season of 40 days before *Easter*, which echoes the 40 days *Jesus* spent *fasting* in the desert. Fasting is more strictly observed in the *Orthodox churches*, but some kind of abstinence, or extra religious study or *spiritual* exercise, is observed by most devout Christians during Lent

Leviticus [book of] (Jewish)   A book of the *Pentateuch*, containing ritual rules and advice on healthcare

Liberal synagogue   Liberal Judaism was founded in 1902 as a British Jewish reform movement offering a simplified, universalistic and contemporary form of worship and practice and emphasising ethical dimensions (see also *Progressive Judaism*)

liturgy   A formal pattern of worship

London City Mission (Christian)   An organisation of Christian *evangelists* working in London

Lotus Sutra (Buddhist)   One of the most important sutras (writings) of the Mahayana branch of Buddhism, emphasizing the compassion of the *Buddha* and interpreting him as a divine being with supernatural powers

Luke (Saint)/Luke's Gospel (Christian)   Luke was a physician and travelling companion of *Paul*; his *Gospel*, the third in the *New Testament*, is based on *Mark*'s *Gospel* and other writings

Makkah/Mecca (Muslim)   The birthplace of the *Prophet Muhammad*; the holy city in Saudi Arabia where the annual *Hajj* (pilgrimage) takes place and towards which Muslims face when they pray

mala (Hindu, Sikh, Buddhist)   A string of prayer beads used to aid concentration when praying or meditating

mandala (Buddhist/Hindu) Complicated diagrams or models of the universe, based on ancient designs, which are made to symbolise the order and harmony of an enlightened mind. Used particularly in *meditation*

mandir (Hindu) The building (also called *temple*) wherein the images (*murti*) of gods and goddesses reside and the devotees come to worship

Mark (Saint)/Mark's Gospel (Christian) The second and oldest of the four *Gospels* in the *New Testament*

Mass (Christian) Another word for *Eucharist*. A term particularly used by Roman Catholics

Mataji (Hindu and Sikh) Literally 'Mother dear', a common name for mother and also used as a devotional reference to a female deity (called more formally 'Shakhti')

Matthew (Saint)/Matthew's Gospel (Christian) He was one of Jesus' twelve *disciples* and a tax collector by profession. The first book of the *New Testament* is attributed to him

meditation 'Mindfulness': the practice of achieving tranquillity with awareness of the present moment, or an 'emptying' of the mind, or the focusing of the mind on an object or on the Divine. Meditation is important in at least some strands of every religion, and is especially central to Buddhism

Methodist Church A Christian *denomination* deriving from the preaching and teaching of *John Wesley* and his brother Charles in the eighteenth century, with their emphasis on a methodical pursuit of Biblical holiness and *hymn* singing

Micah (Jewish) A Hebrew *prophet* and book in the *Hebrew Bible*

minister (Christian) The word used for *ordained* men and women, particularly in the *Free Churches*

mission (Christian) Going out to serve and teach the *gospel*. Missionaries are the people who do this

Mohammed see *Muhammad*

monk/monastic (1) In Christianity a monk is a man committed to God through a life of prayer, austerity and discipline. Monks usually live in community with other monks in a monastery. They may go out to teach the faith and to do various kinds of social work. (2) Monks are central to Buddhism. The '*Sangha*' (community of monks) system varies in different Buddhist traditions. They are the repositories and the expounders of the 'Dharma' – the teachings of the *Buddha* – and as such are revered and supported (in practical ways) by the Buddhist *laity*

monotheism Belief that there is one God/Divinity/Ultimate Being/ Supreme Spirit

Monsignor (Mgr) (Christian) An honorific designation given to some *Roman Catholic priests*

mosque or masjid (Muslim) A place of assembly for prayer and worship. Most mosques have a dome and a minaret (tower) from which (in Islamic countries) the faithful are called to prayer

Muhammad (Prophet) (570–632 CE) (Muslim)   Islam's final *prophet* and messenger, and the one through whom the *Qur'an* was revealed from *Allah* (God). His life was centred on Makkah and Medina in (Saudi) Arabia. (See also *pbuh*)

multi faith   Activity in which institutions and/or members of different religions are involved together, e.g. in *chaplaincy*. See Chapter 1

murti (Hindu)   The embodied or visualised forms of the infinite deity; the 'statues' of gods and goddesses to be found in Hindu *mandirs* (*temples*) and homes

New Testament (Christian)   The second part of the *Bible*. A collection of books written soon after *Jesus*' death and *resurrection*. The four *Gospels* narrate Jesus' life, death and resurrection; the *Acts of the Apostles* records the birth of the *Church*; there are letters to various churches from early apostles; and the book of *Revelation*, a series of apocalyptic visions

Nipponzan Myohoji (Buddhist)   A Japanese Buddhist revival movement founded in 1917 by Fujii Nichidatsu, based on the teachings of Nichirin (a thirteenth-century Japanese *monk*). *Meditation* on the *Lotus Sutra* is central. Known for its worldwide marches for peace and for its Peace *Pagodas* built around the world

niqab (Muslim)   A face veil worn by women which covers all but their eyes

nun   See *monk*. A nun is the female equivalent (approximately) to a monk; Christian nuns usually live together in a 'convent'. In Buddhism there are far fewer nuns than monks

office (Christian)   The daily prayers prescribed in *liturgical churches* of which Morning and Evening Prayer are the most commonly used now. Originated in the monasteries in the sixth century when there were eight fixed daily hours for prayer. (Five or more of these offices are still used by *monks* and *nuns* in monasteries and convents.) The offices include *psalms, hymns, Bible* readings, prayers and other elements

ordinand   A person in training for *ordination*

ordination   For Christians, the act of making someone a *deacon, priest* or *bishop*. At a special service, a bishop lays his hands on each candidate and prays that God's Spirit will give them the necessary grace in their future ministry. The term 'ordination' is also used for the ceremony at which Buddhist *monks* are formally admitted to the *Sangha*, but there are significant differences in the concept of ordination: e.g. Buddhist ordination is not necessarily for life. In *Judaism*, 'ordination' is the ceremony in which *rabbis* are officially granted their qualification

Orthodox Church   One of the major and oldest branches of Christ-

ianity, which includes the Russian, Greek and Serbian Orthodox
Churches. Each Church has its own Patriarch (leader); the Ecumenical
Patriarch of Constantinople is recognised as the most senior. Ortho-
dox means 'right teaching' or traditional

Orthodox synagogue   The term 'Orthodox' was first applied to
Judaism in 1795 to distinguish it from the Jewish *Reform* movement.
Orthodox Jews adhere strictly to the laws contained in the Hebrew
Scriptures and to the tradition founded on them

pagoda (Buddhist)   A structure developed in the Far East, from the
Indian 'stupa', which contains relics of a/the *Buddha* or a famous
teacher/master. Usually tall with prominent eaves, every part of the
structure has a symbolic meaning

Palm Sunday (Christian)   The Sunday a week before *Easter* Day when
Christians recall *Jesus'* entry into Jerusalem at the beginning of the
week before his *crucifixion* and *resurrection*. The crowd that welcomed
him strewed the road with palm branches; and worshippers today are
given *crosses* made of palm fronds

parish (Christian)   A district with its *church* (or churches) and all the
people who live there, for which a *priest* (or team of priests) has *spiritual* and *pastoral* responsibility

Parish Communion   See *Eucharist*

Parochial Church Council (PCC)   The governing body of a *parish*. The
churchwardens and the *incumbent* are ex officio members. Members are
elected from the electoral roll at the Annual Parochial Church
Meeting. The Council takes all decisions relating to the life of the
parish except for a few reserved to the incumbent (mainly in relation
to the conduct of worship)

pastoral   Anything to do with the *spiritual* care and well-being of the
people in a geographical area or in an institution such as a hospital,
college or prison. In the Christian tradition, 'pastoral' has analogy
with the way a shepherd looks after sheep (often referred to in the
teaching of *Jesus*)

Patriarch   (1) Title for the leaders of the different Eastern *Orthodox
Churches*. (2) Patriarchs and matriarchs: the ancestors of the Jewish
people, e.g. *Abraham* and his wife Sarah

Paul (Saint) (Christian)   The most important early Christian *missionary*, apostle and theologian, and author of a number of books in the
New Testament. These are letters to various *churches* he had visited on
his missionary journeys and are the foundation for much of later
Christian *theology*

(pbuh) Peace be upon him (Muslim)   Often written or spoken by
(English-speaking) Muslims after the name *Prophet Muhammad* and
after *Jesus* and other prophets, as a sign of the honour in which they
are held

penitence   Repenting of sins (wrong doings); seeking of forgiveness.

Penitential seasons are *Lent* (before *Easter*) and *Advent* (before *Christmas*) for Christians; the ten days before *Yom Kippur* for Jews; and the month of *Ramadan* for Muslims

Pentateuch   The first five books (Genesis, Exodus, Leviticus, Numbers and Deuteronomy) of the Hebrew Scriptures containing the history of the Jewish people from the creation of the world to the death of Moses. Known as the *Torah*. For Christians they are the first books of the part of the *Bible* known as the 'Old Testament'

Pentecost   A Jewish festival (also called Shavu'ot). At this festival, 50 days after the first *Easter, Jesus' disciples* experienced the coming of the *Holy Spirit* to empower them to preach the good news of his *resurrection* and his message of God's love for everyone. This event is celebrated by Christians today seven weeks after Easter on 'Pentecost' or 'Whitsunday'

Pentecostal (Christian)   A Christian revivalist movement that emerged first in the USA, in the late nineteenth century. Central to their prayer and worship are the gifts of the *Holy Spirit* mentioned by *Paul* in his first *letter to the Corinthians*, chapters 12 and 14 (wisdom, knowledge, miraculous healing powers, *baptism* in the Spirit, and particularly speaking in tongues and interpretation of God's message). Worship is characterised by hand clapping, raised arms, dance and prophecy

Peter (Saint) (Christian)   One of *Jesus'* first *disciples*

pilgrim   A person who makes a journey to a *sacred* place for religious reasons

prasad (Hindu)   Food offerings to the deities, which are then shared, as a blessing, among worshippers

presbyter (Christian)   Greek word for 'elder', connoting both age and wisdom. The term is used in the *New Testament* for Christians in leadership positions, and in many *churches* today it continues to have this meaning

priest   A religious functionary with prescribed rights and responsibilities. The meaning of the term, and the rights and responsibilities attached to it, differ in the different religions

Progressive Judaism   A collective term to refer to non-*Orthodox* branches of *Judaism* such as *Reform* and *Liberal*. Differences from the Orthodox include choral singing in worship and prayers in the vernacular (as well as Hebrew), the *ordination* of women *rabbis* and the relaxation of dietary laws (*kosher*)

prophet   A person who is able, more than most, to divine the will of God and reveal it to others. Many of the prophets of the *Hebrew Bible* (The Old Testament for Christians) are also the prophets of *Islam*

proselytisation   The attempt to persuade someone to be *converted* to a religion

Proverbs [book of]   A book of ancient wisdom contained in the *Hebrew Bible*

Psalms [book of]   A collection of 150 ancient Hebrew *hymns* in the

Hebrew Bible. Also much used in Christian *congregational* and private worship

puja/poojah (Hindu, Buddhist, Jain)   Meaning respect, homage, worship. The act of puja has countless variations but usually includes offering gifts (flowers, food and/or money) to a deity; or, in the case of Buddhists, in homage to the *Buddha*. Devout Hindus perform puja once or twice a day in the *temple* or at home

qiblah (Muslim)   The direction of *Makkah* towards which Muslims face to pray. In a *mosque* it is marked by a niche or alcove in the wall, called a mihrab

Quaker   A religious group of Christian derivation, established during the seventeenth century by George Fox. Known as The (Religious) Society of Friends, they have no formal *creed*, religious hierarchy or *ordained* ministry. There is an emphasis on attentive silence in worship and on non-violence (pacifism) and social action for the poor and disadvantaged. They are often involved in *inter faith* engagement

Qur'an (Muslim)   Muslim *sacred* text, written in Arabic, and containing the *revelation* received by the *Prophet Muhammad* from *Allah* (God)

rabbi (Jewish)   A *spiritual* leader and teacher of a Jewish community

Ramadan (Muslim)   The ninth month of the Islamic year, when Muslims *fast* from dawn till dusk – to give thanks for the *Qur'an* (which was first revealed in the month of Ramadan), to practise self-control, and to identify with the poor and hungry of the world

reader (Christian)   A *lay person*, in the C. of E., trained in *theology* and preaching and in leading worship (but not the *Eucharist*) and licensed by the *bishop* to fulfil these functions in a *parish* or parishes

rector (Christian)   In the C. of E., one of the two designations of an *incumbent* of a *parish*. The other is *'vicar'*. Historically the vicar stood in for a rector

Reform Judaism   A movement originating in the eighteenth century in Germany, which emphasised the importance of harmonious integration into general society. In the UK, Reform groupings emerged in the 1940s in distinction to the existing *Liberal* congregations. See also *Progressive Judaism*

Remembrance Sunday   The Sunday nearest to 11 November, on which date the armistice at the end of the First World War in 1918 took effect. A two-minute silence is observed at 11 a.m. to remember all those who have died in war

resurrection   (1) The belief, especially in *Christianity* and *Islam*, in restoration to a new life, in a new dimension, after death. (2) The resurrection of *Jesus*; the fundamental Christian belief that Jesus died on the *cross* and that God raised him to new life

revelation   (1) What God reveals, through a *prophet*, a *sacred* text, human experience, or in other ways. (2) The book of Revelation (a series of apocalyptic visions) is the name of the last book of the *New Testament*

ritual Ceremonial activity which varies hugely, but usually entails repetition, commitment, intention, pattern, traditional elements, purpose and performance

Roman Catholic Church All those dioceses worldwide that are in *communion* with the *Bishop* of Rome (the Pope). Its headquarters are in the Vatican in Rome

Sabbath/Shabbat (Hebrew) The Jewish day of rest and congregational worship, from sunset on Friday to sunset on Saturday

sacrament (Christian) An outward and visible sign of an inward *spiritual* grace. The *Church of England* recognises two sacraments: *baptism* and the *Eucharist*. *Orthodox* and *Roman Catholic* traditions recognise five more solemn religious acts as sacraments: *confirmation*, penance, extreme unction (administered just before death), *ordination* and marriage

SACRE The Standing Advisory Council for Religious Education appointed by each local authority. It should include representatives of the different religious communities in the area. Its task includes determining the local RE syllabus and monitoring the teaching of RE in local schools

sacred Holy; set apart for a particular religious purpose

Saint (Christian) Title given to exemplary Christians; they may be venerated and invoked in prayer (see also *All Saints*)

'Salaam aleikum' (Arabic) 'Peace be upon you' (plural). Common greeting in Islamic communities

Salah/salat (Muslim) Muslim formal prayer (in Arabic), five times a day. One of the Five Pillars of *Islam*. 'Namaz' is the Urdu word for Salah

Salvation Army (Christian) A Christian organisation, founded in 1865 by William Booth, with an emphasis on *evangelism* and social care

Samaritans (1) Inhabitants of the area around Samaria, north of Jerusalem, for several centuries before and during *Jesus'* lifetime. There was animosity between them and the Jews. They worshipped God according to their version of the *Pentateuch*. (2) Name of a Christian organisation founded by Chad Varah in 1953 to support people who are tempted to commit suicide

Sangha (Buddhist) (1) The communities of *monks* and *nuns* and of *lay* men and women – the fourfold Sangha. (2) One of 'The Three Jewels' of Buddhism: the teacher (*Buddha*), his teachings (Dharma) and his followers (Sangha) in which Buddhists 'take refuge' as a daily act of commitment

Sanskrit (Hindu) The ancient language in which the oldest Hindu *sacred* books are written

sect A religious organisation set up in distinction from, and often in protest against, an established religion

server (Christian) Someone who assists a *priest* in *church* during the *Eucharist*

shalwar kameez A long tunic shirt (kameez) worn over baggy trousers (shalwar), by men and women from Asian backgrounds

Shari'a (Muslim) Means 'pathway'. The framework that codifies Islamic values as they apply to all aspects of life. It is based primarily on the *Qur'an* and the 'hadith' (traditions concerning the words and actions of the *Prophet Muhammad* and his companions). Interpretation and implementation of Shari'a law varies widely in the Islamic world and there are a number of different schools of Islamic law

Shi'a (Muslim) The branch of *Islam* (about one tenth of the world's Muslims) that follows the succession of leadership from the family of the *Prophet Muhammad*. Basic beliefs and daily religious practices are similar to that of *Sunni* Islam

Shiva (Hindu) One of the three greatest Hindu gods (the other two are Brahma and Vishnu). Lord Shiva is worshipped as the regenerator god who watches over death and rebirth, and as the Lord of the (cosmic) Dance

shrine A *sacred* place where people worship, pray or *meditate*

Sikhism The religion that began in the Punjab area of India, with the teaching of *Guru Nanak* (1469–1539). He was followed by nine more *Gurus*, the last being Guru Gobind Singh who instituted the *Khalsa* in 1699. Since his death, *spiritual* authority resides in the *Guru Granth Sahib*, the holy book that contains the teachings of the Gurus (and others)

Singh/Kaur (Sikh) Sikh men have Singh (lion) as their second name and women have Kaur (princess), to identify them as Sikhs, as decreed by the tenth *Guru* in 1699. (Note: not all men called Singh are Sikh)

SLIFG South London Inter Faith Group: www.southlondoninterfaith.org.uk

soul An indefinable element of a person that is, nevertheless, able to respond to holiness and the *spiritual* dimension. In the belief of many religious people the soul continues after bodily death

spiritual capital A network of *spiritual* relationships (within, outside and between *congregations*) and of spiritual capabilities (of individuals and communities) on which individuals and communities can draw for their spiritual needs

spiritual The capacity to recognise and respond to the non-material, including the *sacred*, dimension of human life

Stations of the Cross (Christian) Fourteen pictures or carvings placed in a sequence in a *church*, showing different stages of *Jesus'* journey to his *crucifixion* through the streets of Jerusalem

Sunni (Muslim) The majority (90 per cent) of the world's Muslims are of the Sunni tradition. The split between Sunnis and *Shi'as* came after the death of the *Prophet Muhammad* and is related to who should be the authoritative leaders of *Islam*

surah/sura (Muslim)   A division (chapter) of the *Qur'an*. There are 114 surahs of varying length

synagogue or shul (Jewish)   A Jewish 'meeting house' for *congregational* worship, prayer, teaching, study, and cultural and social activities

synod (Christian)   A gathering of elected and ex officio members for deliberation and decision-making. The *Church of England* has synods at the *parish* level (Parochial Church Council), the Deanery level (Deanery Synod), the Diocesan level (Diocesan Synod), and the national level (General Synod)

temple   A place in which to worship. (1) Used loosely to describe a Hindu *mandir*, a Sikh *gurdwara* or a Buddhist vihara. (2) For Jews, Temple means the historic Temple in Jerusalem, of which one wall still stands (known as the Western or 'Wailing' Wall) and which remains a very significant focus for devout Jews

theology   The study of God. ('theos' is Greek for God, and 'logos' means word or discourse)

Torah (Jewish)   Holy Scriptures (see *Pentateuch*)

turban (Sikh)   A length of fine cloth wound into a head dress. Devout Sikhs do not cut their hair (one of the *Five Ks* is 'kesh' – uncut hair). The turban is worn mainly by men (but also by some women) as a sign of Sikh identity. (Note: not all men who wear turbans are Sikhs)

United Reformed Church   A Christian *denomination*. A *Free Church* formed in 1972 from a merger of the Congregational Church and the Presbyterian Church in England, both of which date from the sixteenth century

Upanishads (Hindu)   One of the major early Hindu scriptures with philosophical and *meditative* material

vicar (Christian)   One of the two designations of an *incumbent* of an *Anglican parish*. He or she has responsibility for the *church* and worship, and *pastoral* care for the people within the parish boundaries. (The other is *'rector'*)

vocation   A sense of being called by God to a particular task

wudu (Muslim)   Ablutions or ritual washing (of hands, face, hair, mouth, nose, arms and feet) before all prayers. Wudu facilities are available in a *mosque*

Yom Kippur or 'Day of Atonement' (Jewish)   The end of the solemn ten days of repentance (which starts with Rosh Hashanah, the Jewish New Year) in September/October. Yom Kippur is a day of *fasting*, prayer and worship, and of seeking forgiveness from one another and from God

Zoroastrian   The religion of the followers of the *prophet* Zarathustra (called Zoroaster in the west) around 1200 BC in NE Iran. It was the imperial religion of the Persian empires from 559 BC to AD 652. The main Zoroastrian communities today are in Iran and in India (where they are known as Parsis), although many have migrated to the west.